HAUNTED BLOOMINGTON, INDIANA

HAUNTED BLOOMINGTON, INDIANA

KLARA LEE SWEET

Published by Haunted America
A Division of The History Press
Charleston, SC
www.historypress.com

First published 2021

Manufactured in the United States

ISBN 9781467149969

Library of Congress Control Number: 2021941052

Notice: The information in this book is true and complete to the best of our knowledge. It is offered without guarantee on the part of the author or The History Press. The author and The History Press disclaim all liability in connection with the use of this book.

For my loving husband and best friend, for never giving up on me and believing in me. You have continuously supported me in everything I do. I love you.

Love is the one thing we're capable of perceiving that transcends dimensions of time and space. Maybe we should trust that, even if we can't understand it.

For my dad and lifelong friend. I know you're with me and proud, as you were with anything I did. I'm sure you would've loved this book and stuck it proudly in a frame. I miss you every day.

For my beloved best friend, Ginny. I'll never forget your unwavering, unconditional love and companionship over the last half of my life. Until we meet again.

CONTENTS

Contents

ACKNOWLEDGEMENTS

My love of the strange and unusual wouldn't exist had I not been introduced to the works of Alvin Schwartz, R.L. Stine, Stephen King and Tim Burton at a very young age. It's R.L. Stine I owe my love of reading to, as my first Goosebumps book, *The Beast from the East*, was thrown into my hand at the early age of five or six. I couldn't put it down, and I still own it proudly.

The inspiration for this book came from other Haunted America books by The History Press and from Alvin Schwartz, whose *Scary Stories to Tell in the Dark* series was purchased for me by my parents. Those scary stories were the first horror works I read, and ever since, I'm easily entertained by stories of this nature.

I'm overwhelmingly grateful for my best friend, Lauren, for allowing me to send her running all over town to capture the photographs I needed for this book. Without her, I would have floundered, and finishing this book would not have been possible. Thank you for always participating in whatever shenanigans I cook up.

Without my loving and supportive husband, I may have given up on this idea when I hit a roadblock. Thank you for being so sure I could reach my requirements when I thought they were unreachable. You continue to act like it's a no-brainer that I'll achieve my goals, and I appreciate that. You gave me the confidence I needed.

Thank you so much, Rodrick and Sydney from the Indiana Memorial Union. You were so gracious when I called you up at the last second, and I appreciate that.

Acknowledgements

Without the assistance of Dina Kellams of the Indiana University Archives, who volunteered her time to scan dozens of documents from the archives, this book would not have been possible. I would like to recognize Jennifer Wiggins of the *Indiana Daily Student* and Hilary Fleck at the Monroe County History Center for supplying the photographs that showcased the beauty of Bloomington.

Thank you, Matthew from Paraholics Indiana, for stepping in and capturing photographs of Rose Hill Cemetery when I had hit a wall.

Stephanie Huber of HUBERart has produced the stunning sketches of various buildings and monuments throughout Bloomington, which are appreciatively used throughout this publication. You can see all of her artwork on Etsy.

Many thanks to the following for your personal phone interviews, all of which I truly enjoyed. You are what made this book, and I can't thank you enough: Megan MacDonald of the Monroe County Historical Center; Royal Hair Salon's Madison; Johnna Stepler and Seanin at the Irish Lion; Matthew of Paraholics, who was just as excited about this book as I was; and Kristina Downs of the *Journal of Folklore Research* at Indiana University. I enjoyed hearing all of your firsthand experiences and appreciated you sharing your knowledge of the locations noted in this book. Thank you all so very much!

INTRODUCTION

Monroe County is home to sprawling cemeteries, caves, old limestone quarries and dense forests, teeming with wildlife. The majority of the oldest buildings in town were constructed using the locally quarried limestone, which Bloomington is known for. In fact, limestone is such a critical part of Indiana's history, success and growth that Indiana is known as the "Limestone State." In past decades, limestone quarries were so successful and employed thousands of people, known as "cutters." This is briefly touched on in the movie *Breaking Away*, which won an Academy Award and a Golden Globe. Bloomington quarries were also used as a reference for the Netflix show *Stranger Things*.

Bloomington, which gets its name from the abundance of blooms the settlers were impressed with, was established in 1818. Just thirty families from Kentucky, Tennessee, the Carolinas and Virginia founded the city, and they relied heavily on each other for lumber, gristmills, wool, distilleries and tanneries. Between 1830 and 1840, the stagecoach was introduced, thus improving the transportation of goods from Ohio to Indianapolis. Highways and river canals were constructed to give traders access to the Ohio and the Mississippi River routes, allowing for the trading of goods from out of state. In the 1850s, a railroad brought and shipped produce from markets, and Bloomington's businesses prospered. Saloons, pubs and hotels started sprouting up, along with commercial buildings around the downtown square.

Bloomington Railroad Tracks. *Courtesy of FillyFoto.*

At the very heart of the downtown square, where the stately courthouse stands, many of these old building have kept their two-hundred-year old appearances and are now occupied by local retail shops, restaurants, coffee shops and bakeries. The courthouse was established in the late 1800s and has a gleaming copper dome on top, with a weathervane in the shape of a fish, which symbolizes Christianity. Roughly 360 to 325 million years ago, Bloomington sat on the edge of a sea. The clay-abundant areas of the Hoosier National Forest reveal prehistoric fossils of fish and aquatic plants. These fossils, called crinoids, are discovered in copious amounts, as the sedimentary limestone found all over the state is perfect for the preservation of fossils.

Indiana is the birthplace of a good number of talented innovators, such as Mick Mars and Michael Jackson; however, Bloomington boasts natives including David Lee Roth, Joshua Bell, Mick Foley, Bobby Helms and Johnny "Cougar" Mellencamp. Indiana University's (IU) *Nutcracker*, which won an Emmy Award for its documentary, *Sugarplum Dreams: Staging the Nutcracker Ballet*, performs in Bloomington every December at the Musical Arts Center. The Buskirk Chumley IU Auditorium and Jacobs School of Music offers a wide range of entertainment, such as operas and orchestra concerts, Broadway musicals, standup comedians and theater productions. The Sidney and Lois Eskenazi Museum of Art holds artifacts from Africa, Asia and ancient Egypt and art dating from 30,000 BCE through 1000 CE.

Those who are in search of outdoor adventures can find the peace or adventure they're looking for in Bloomington, as there are three major lakes, perfect for fishing, boating and wildlife watching. The Hoosier National Forest provides the best hiking and horseback riding trails, camp sites and hunting grounds. Bobcats, coyotes, wild turkeys, fox, deer and a large variety of birds can be found in the woods of Monroe County, and "mushroom hunting" is even an activity done here.

For many, the scariest thing that comes to mind when thinking about Bloomington, Indiana, may be the imagery of IU basketball coach Bobby Knight angrily lifting a chair over his head; yet, for all its bright spots, Bloomington harbors spine-tingling secrets. Many stories of urban legends and fascinating folklore span decades and even centuries. A handful of Hoosiers have appeared relieved to release their untold stories from events that have occurred in recent years, as they were previously too weary to come forth with what they've seen and heard for fear of negative judgment. Finally, we may hear their stories that coincide with the legends of old

View of downtown Bloomington and its courthouse. *Courtesy of White Iron Images.*

Cedar Ford Reconstructed Covered Bridge in rural Monroe County, Indiana. *Courtesy of Kenneth Keifer, 2018.*

within Bloomington. Once one learns the history of the locations and the legends passed down from the elders, it's undeniable that Bloomington has earned a reputation for the paranormal. As with most local legends, most of the stories exist today thanks to word-of-mouth storytelling, although more recent accounts of unexplained phenomena continue to be shared by the locals.

IU folklore professor Linda Degh once spoke to around fifty IU students at the Teter Quadrangle about spirits and the supernatural. She claimed there could be several reasons why a spirit still lingers on Earth and why they can't seem to move on to the afterlife. One argument is that the spirits may not actually be aware that they've died, but instead, they continue to exist as they had while they were still living by carrying out what was normal to them in their lives. Degh additionally believes that spirits may linger due to unfinished business. This means that if the departed had something in their life that was important to them, yet unaccomplished, they couldn't be able to move on into the afterlife. Her third reason for a soul being withheld from eternal rest is if they perished before it was their natural time to die or if they died in a horrific way.

IU folklore professors have also stated these as possible reasons for the existence of ghosts. They, like so many other folklore specialists and professors, advise that spirits may also have the abilities to manifest in multiple forms. Some consider the idea that the supernatural may have the ability to choose how they appear to the living, if at all. Many business owners, cemetery managers and homeowners in Bloomington are open to the idea of spirits existing among us, even if they've never seen or heard them.

1
Indiana University

I don't think I have ever been at a more beautiful university commencement than this. I shall always keep in mind this scene here in the open…here under these great trees, these maples and beeches, that have survived over from the primeval forest.
—U.S. president Theodore Roosevelt during his June 12, 1918 IU commencement speech

Indiana Memorial Union

At the very heart of Indiana University's campus, once rated one of the most beautiful campuses in the United States, looms an impressive, castle-like structure. Spanning one-fifth of a mile from the east end to the west, it's constructed of the same limestone as many other IU buildings. The construction of the building began in 1931 and was completed in 1932. Until the tower on the west end of the building was erected in 1954, the Indiana Memorial Union (IMU) was once part of the Biddle Hotel—added in 1960—and reception room, which is still around today.

When this portion was completed, this area became the popular social place on campus, teeming with students and visitors, due to there not being many local bars or restaurants at the time. Although the impressive building was finished in the early 1930s, the true beginning of the union came in early 1900s, when the hostility between fraternity students and off-campus pupils, as well as between freshmen and sophomores, hit its peak. John

Whittenberger sparked the idea for the Indiana Memorial Union with the goal of encouraging a peaceful unification among its students by forming the Men's Union in 1909.

The monumental structure receives over fifteen thousand people on a daily basis and up to twenty-three thousand during the first semester of the school year. Under one roof, the IMU offers a Starbucks, bowling alley, food court, study areas, a salon, a movie theater, shopping areas and more. It's even home to the Biddle Hotel, where visitors can stay the night in the very heart of campus in one of the coziest rooms you'll find in Bloomington. When arriving at the main entrance and going through the revolving door, a stone staircase is lined with large portraits and leads up to the second floor.

The largest painting is the portrait of former chancellor and president of IU Herman B. Wells, leaning forward and watching over those who arrive and leave the building. Before climbing the stairs on your left, the opening on the first floor leads to the cozy lobby for the Biddle Hotel on your right. The lobby features oversized leather armchairs and gorgeous wooden wall paneling. The union looks akin to a castle, with its looming stone tower, a staircase hosting giant paintings and branching corridors. It appears to be more than one hundred years old. It's also home to numerous haunts.

Opposite: The Sample Gates was built as the iconic entrance to Indiana University. Rated one of the most beautiful college campuses in the United States, IU Bloomington also holds a haunted history at almost every one of its corners. *Courtesy of Lauren Clark, 2021.*

Above: Indiana Memorial Union. *Courtesy of Lauren Clark, 2021.*

Perhaps the striking number of strange sightings and disembodied sounds there is due to the fact that the five hundred thousand square foot building sits in the middle of the oldest part of IU's 1,940-acre campus. A growling phantom dog wanders the hallways and areas around the outside of the building, only to run into bushes and shadows without ever being caught or found again. No one knows why this phantom dog hangs around the IMU; however, some have reported seeing it, and one story told of a dog that had jumped out of one of the windows, causing the spirit of the dog to remain on the grounds. Random cold spots, yelling heard down the empty halls after closing hours, human figures falling from the roof in the night, haunted paintings and a haunted elevator are the strange occurrences that happen in this unique building. While there are many accounts of staff, maintenance workers and students seeing and hearing paranormal presences, they are fortunately nonthreatening; although they are pretty frightening at times.

Haunted Paintings of the Tudor Room and Federal Room

Even if you're not a believer in ghosts, visiting Indiana University's Memorial Union is worth the time if you enjoy art and architecture. The IMU is home to many paintings within all of its one-hundred-year-old hallways, offices and rooms, many of which are portraits of long-passed Hoosiers who continue to keep an eye on the university's students. Several of these portraits are believed to be haunted.

One of the most chilling paintings is that of a young boy holding a jack-o'-lantern. Always referred to as Jacob, the sweet-looking boy in O.O. Haig's 1938 portrait titled *Halloween* hangs in the attractive Tudor Room on one of the upper floors. Fifteenth-century tapestries hang overhead, beautiful paintings are displayed on almost all of the walls and dining tables are set with white cloths and delicately placed dishes. In the painting, Jacob appears to have a "forced" smile that little boys might have when their parents beg them to pose for a photograph they're not interested in holding still for.

Like most little boys, Jacob is mischievous, according to the Tudor Room staff and students. Legend has it that after this painting was completed, the little boy in O.O. Haig's portrait died in a fire and returned to his painting in the afterlife. According to the Indiana Memorial Union's Facebook page, staff have dealt with the mischievous little boy's pranks, as he's known more as a prankster than an evil spirit. Staff would set tables up in preparation for the next day and lock up, only to find the room in disarray the next morning. Flowers, glasses and tablecloths would be knocked over, shattered or scattered on the floor.

Before closing hours, staff members wrap the silverware in napkins and set them carefully at their place settings. Employees have stated that on unlocking and entering the room the next day, the silverware has been unwrapped and scattered all over the tables on multiple occasions. When the room is found in disarray, the cause is usually pinned on the little boy in the painting. This has been known to be especially true when big changes have been made to the room, such as when the large hanging tapestries are removed yearly for cleaning.

Due to the fact that the tapestries are old and made of delicate material, they must be sent away for professional cleaning, which can sometimes take a couple of weeks. Tudor Room employees have said that after removing the tapestries and sending them off for their yearly cleaning, they have found tremendous wrecks in the room that are larger than the small pranks Jacob usually leaves. The silverware has been undone and scattered again,

O.O. Haig's "Halloween" painting hangs in the Tutor Room. Jacob, who is shown in this portrait, perished in a house fire not long after this was painted. *Courtesy of Lauren Clark, 2021.*

The medieval tapestries that hang from the paneled ceiling in the Tudor Room must be a favorite of Jacob's, the ghost boy. *Courtesy of Lauren Clark, 2021.*

dishes and glasses have been shattered, tables have been overturned and the tablecloths have been removed and piled in the corner of the room, creating what I can imagine to be an upsetting amount of cleanup the next day. The vandalism immediately ceases as soon as the tapestries are returned and rehung. It seems that Jacob prefers his room to remain just the way it is.

The *Halloween* portrait isn't the only haunted portrait in the building. On the second floor in the beautiful Colonial Williamsburg–style Federal Room hangs the unfinished portrait of Mary Quick Burney over the fireplace. The wallpaper is the same print that's used in the Diplomatic Reception Room of the White House. A pioneer of the art movement at Indiana University and a member of the Art Committees of General and State Federations of Clubs, Mary Burney passed away in 1933, before her portrait was even finished. The story is that Mary was extremely dissatisfied with the way her portrait was being painted by Wayman Adams. She was aware that her portrait was going to join the portraits of others who had performed great achievements at the IMU. She raised quite a stir within the university when she began looking around for a replacement painter. Since she passed away before the painting was finished, it's believed that she continues to haunt the Federal Room, where it's displayed.

Perhaps the painting was her unfinished business, since it was the one thing we knew she was unhappy about right before her death. Staff who have felt a never-ending presence in this room have declared that doors unlock as they are performing their nightly lock-up, as if someone is following right behind them, unlocking the doors they have just secured. In fact, this ordeal has become so common that staff have been instructed to perform a double-check before leaving for the night.

Poor Mary had suffered devastating losses in her life. Her husband passed away before her, and she had lost her son in a fire sometime later. Over the mantel in the Federal Room hangs her portrait, flanked by two urns—one holding her husband's ashes and the other holding her son's. Oddly, in June 2001, one of the two urns went missing. The urn was lost for years, and, just as mysteriously as it disappeared, it reappeared one day on the mantel where it used to be. Visitors have smelled perfume when entering the room, often described as the smell of roses or other flowers that were extremely aged. Others often note the faint smell of smoke, as if a candle has just been blown out, although there are no candles within the room. Could this be Mary's perfume or the smoke from the fire that killed her son the guests are smelling?

Left: The interior of the Colonial Williamsburg–style Federal Room. *Courtesy of Lauren Clark, 2021.*

Below: The lovely portrait of Mary Quick Burney flanked by detailed urns, which hold the ashes of her husband and son. *Courtesy of Lauren Clark, 2021.*

The Ghost Tower

Walking near the west end of the Indiana Memorial Union at night, strollers may witness an unsettling sight. Be wary when looking upward at the eight-story west tower, known as the "Ghost Tower" or the "Tower of Terror." Students walking on the sidewalk below have seen a black, shadowy figure plummeting from the top, toward the sidewalk below, only to vanish before the figure reaches the ground.

This recurring moment may have something to do with a grim event that took place decades ago, when the West Tower was once part of the Biddle Hotel. In 1960, a man who had lost his job and battling health issues visited for an interview and stayed on the fifth floor of the hotel. As the story goes, the interview didn't go well, and the other interviewees were insulting him. One night, he either took the elevator or climbed the stairs to the eighth floor of the tower and jumped through a window. While some believe the man chose suicide, others think he may have been pushed, since he had supposedly made enemies during his visit. Either way, he died immediately on making contact with the ground. Perhaps the shadowy, human-shaped figure falling from the top of the tower belongs to the soul of this man.

In the wee hours between 2:00 and 6:00 a.m., everyone from the building managers to the maintenance workers have heard footsteps walking behind them when no one is around. The sound of moving furniture or laughter, as well as incoherent voices, echoes down hallways and stairwells in the dead of the night. At other times, the voices are clear and easy to understand and have even shouted the names of people. Nothing is ever found when staff investigate, often when they are the only ones in the building. While walking down the hallways of the closed building, a sudden chill is felt, and strange smells are picked up. Perhaps it's only a bird and the dark interior of the rooms playing tricks on the eyes; however, a couple of students and staff have sworn they have looked at windows, only to find a figure falling past, hurtling toward the sidewalk below. Not surprisingly, the figure disappears completely before striking the ground.

On the eighth floor is the beautiful, privately used Bryan Room, where the same type of haunting occurs regularly. Like the Federal Room, the employees working on the eighth floor must turn off all the lights and lock the doors before leaving. The workers do this nightly, descending the stairs or elevator to the bottom floor, going outside and looking up, only to see a light still shining from the Bryan Room. Although one may think this is the result of mere forgetfulness, the last employees will reenter the building,

climb the eight floors, turn all the lights off again and leave to see the lights still shining through the windows. This charade will go on for, at most, five times in a night. It seems as though someone is playing games with the staff, possibly feeling joy watching the poor employees run up and down the tower to turn the light off. Perhaps this is the spirit of the falling man who simply

Opposite: The "Ghost Tower" of the Indiana Memorial Union. *Courtesy of Sart24.*

Right: The Bryan Room is thought to be the most unsettling, creepy room in the building. *Courtesy of Lauren Clark, 2021.*

doesn't wish to be alone in the dark. The elevator even stops and the doors open randomly at the fifth floor when the button isn't pushed.

If these strange happenings at the IMU are all connected to one spirit, it's possible that the poor soul is forever reliving his final moments. The man enters the elevator at the fifth floor, ascends to the eighth floor near the Bryan Room, jumps from the window and hurdles to the sidewalk below, caught in an endless loop. At times, the smell of herbs, recognizable as sage, can be picked up, which some people believe cleanses indoor areas of negative spirits and bad energy. Cold spots can also be felt at random times in locations around the building. Maintenance workers have often been spooked at night when they've heard the sound of footsteps directly behind them after the building is already closed, and the workers turn around to find no one is around.

One summer, a maintenance employee was shutting down the north end of the building, turning off the lights and closing the doors, before turning

The interior of the haunted elevator inside the IMU. *Courtesy of Lauren Clark, 2021.*

around to start the south end of the building. The moment the worker turned around to conduct the lock-up process of the other end of the IMU, a forceful gush of air almost knocked him off his feet. Frightened, the employee turned to see his reflection in the window; however, his wasn't the only reflection he saw. A dark figure was directly behind him, looming over his shoulder. Thinking someone was standing behind him, the man whirled around to find he was alone. At this point, a soft voice, similar to chanting, was heard, and before he decided to investigate further, his walkie-talkie buzzed, and he left quickly.

In 2003 and 2005, Indiana Ghost Trackers, Bloomington Chapter, investigated the Bryan Room along with the rest of the Indiana Memorial Union. Of all the locations within this massive building, more paranormal phenomenon happened within the Bryan Room, including a chair moving on its own and two voice captures on an EVP machine. The ghost trackers declared the Bryan Room the most haunted location in the building.

Dunn Cemetery and the Lady in Black

If there's one thing most IU students wouldn't expect to see at their university, it would be a cemetery, but it's there. Small, old and surrounded by a low, stone wall, Dunn Cemetery was established before Indiana University called this location home. Established by a farmer named George Grundy Dunn in 1855, the little cemetery was built in honor of his grandmother Elinor Brewster Dunn and her two sisters, Agnes "Nancy" Brewster Alexander and Janet Brewster Irvin, who aided the U.S. Army during the Revolutionary War. The three sisters were buried next to each other under one large tombstone.

The Dunn family moved from Virginia to Bloomington in the 1700s. The Dunn family's farmhouse once stood above what is now the location of the HPER Building. Like most of Monroe County, this land was once farmland before it was ever a university, and it was typical for a family farm to have its own family graveyard. George G. Dunn later became a U.S. congressman, and in 1884, his son Moses Dunn sold the twenty acres of land to the IU trustees. This was where IU started, in the twenty acres known as "Dunn Woods," under the strict conditions within the deed:

> *In order to secure and perpetuate to the descendants of Eleanor Dunn, Nancy Alexander, and Jane Irvin, who be buried within the plat of ground…and to those with whom they intermarry, forever a place of private burial, where they shall repose together as one family in the long night of death and rise up together as from one bed at the last day.*

Indiana University has upheld this agreement, since the request to have a burial in Dunn Cemetery is a vigorous process with sorely needed documentation to prove direct ties to the original family. The trees that were included in the deed and that were to remain untouched are still alive and well. One stands inside Dunn Cemetery, and the other is inside the chemistry building, which had to be built around the tree. Today, most students appear not to notice Dunn Cemetery, which they walk by on their way to classes, as the graveyard sits at the crossroads of multiple sidewalks and buildings at the heart of the campus. The crying of babies and children have been heard near this burial site at night, and they grow fainter as one approaches the cemetery's walls.

An infamous ghost story stems from Dunn Cemetery and appeared in its first reference in a local newspaper, issued sometime in 1911. The

Above: Dunn Cemetery. The little Beck Chapel sits next to the graveyard. *Courtesy of Lauren Clark, 2021.*

Left: The headstone for George G. Dunn, who deeded the surrounding land to Indiana University. *Courtesy of Lauren Clark, 2021.*

"Woman in Black," although spotted more often outside the Sample Gates on Indiana Avenue, has been known to haunt this little burial ground. Who the spirit belongs to is a mystery; however, some have speculated that it belongs to one of the Brewster sisters, as she's been spotted gliding from tombstone to tombstone, perhaps tending to the spirits of the soldiers, just as she and her two sisters had done during the Revolutionary War. During the day, the little cemetery is a peaceful, serene place, which looks stunning during autumn, when the leaves change to bright oranges and yellows.

Old Crescent

Never were the university's responsibilities for the development of character of greater significance than at the present hour.
—Herman B. Wells, first inaugural address

At the corner of downtown Bloomington's East Kirkwood Avenue and South Indiana Avenue stands two towering limestone pillars named the Sample Gates. This iconic Bloomington monument marks the gateway into Indiana University's campus. Erected and dedicated in 1987, these iconic pillars were gifted to the university from the former director of the university's Office of Scholarships and Financial Aid Edson Sample. Due to the fact there was much debate between the faculty, staff and students about where the money should be spent, Sample funded the entire construction of the famous structure. With his donation, the university was finally able to acquire this gorgeous entrance to its grounds.

The surrounding garden beds always have flowers that are changed out with the changing seasons to create a beautiful welcome to the university. When walking along the redbrick path through the pillars, one will walk past the some of the campus's oldest and most beautiful stone buildings. The path on the left leads to the Franklin Building, and the right pathway leads straight to Dunn Woods—the old, original woods from the Dunn family's land. The middle path leads to the very heart of IU's campus, through a grassy park-like environment, and another pathway leads up to the Indiana University Memorial Union. Before reaching the union, a seemingly out-of-place, tiny road in the shape of a circle sits between the Frances Morgan Swain Student Building and Maxwell Hall. The road runs past the back side of the union building and stretches up between the

The Sample Gates at the intersection of North Indiana and Kirkwood Avenues. *Courtesy of Lauren Clark, 2021.*

two buildings to form a tiny cul-de-sac with an octagonal-shaped sundial in the middle.

The sundial, now surrounded by an iron fence, was made in 1868 and moved to this spot in 1896. IU graduates from 1886 Mathilde Zwicker and Otto Klophsch were introduced to each other at this spot, fell in love and were later married. When they became elderly, they requested that the university scatter their ashes at the spot where they met and fell in love—around the sundial. IU honored their request when the ashes of Otto were scattered there in 1935, and two years later, the ashes of his widow, Mathilde, were also scattered there.

Nearby is the metal statue of Herman B. Wells, who received his bachelor's degree from IU in 1924, his master's degree in 1927, became a professor in 1930 and dean of the school five years later. In 1937, Wells found himself the acting president of the university until it was made official the following year. Wells was the president of Indiana University for a longer period than any other; however, in 1962, he stepped away to become IU's chancellor. President Wells is still beloved among the

A sketch of Rose Well House in the heart of the IU campus. *Courtesy of Stephanie Huber of HUBERart.*

The inviting statue of the beloved Herman B. Wells, past chancellor, president and professor at IU, welcomes his students and faculty in the oldest part of campus. *Courtesy of Lauren Clark, 2021.*

university and its faculty, staff and students. A friendly statue of him sits on one end of a metal bench, dressed handsomely in a suit, with his tie blowing in the wind, as if frozen in time. He has a friendly smile on his face, and his expression appears to be one of someone seeing an old friend. His right hand is extended outward to welcome new students to the university. His left hand is perched on top of his hat, which sits on the bench next to him.

A student tradition states that if one touches his statue before finals, it will give them good luck. However, IU students have also claimed to have seen Herman B. Wells's statue move. The reports always state that the statue has been spotted moving around at night and sometimes in the early hours of the morning. Although his statue is made of solid metal, students have sworn to find his metal figure waving at them or walking around the Rose Well House or in front of Maxwell Hall, near his bench. Could this be the effects of students returning to campus after a night full of drinking and fun downtown, or could this possibly be President Wells reminding us all that he's still watching over his students and dear university?

Arboretum

A tranquil grassy area of IU Bloomington's campus is known as the Arboretum, where many pathways intersect and lead to other areas of campus. Lush flowers and trees, a small pond, an artistic tower and a charming clock that plays tunes makes this space ideal for studying, picnics, riding one's bicycle and relaxing with friends. This is also the location where, supposedly, a group of friends met every Halloween night to tell scary stories and hold a séance.

Rumor has it, the friend who told the scariest story that night would be the winner. On their final annual gathering before their graduation, the friends laid down blankets, sat in a circle and lit candles. At 10:00 p.m., they sat in the dark and told their stories with the hopes of scaring each other. They were enjoying their spooky time when a strong gust of wind blew out their candles, and a figure faintly appeared before the university students. To their shock, the figure howled at the group, "Get off my lawn!" The terrified group slowly started to back away, and the figure yelled louder, "Get off of my home!"

The students fled the scene and didn't return until the next morning. They found their blankets and the blown-out candles still in place. Nothing seemed

The 162-foot-tall Metz Carillon Tower sits at the intersection of three pathways within the green space of the arboretum. *Courtesy of Lauren Clark, 2021.*

suspicious until they picked up their blankets and, burned into the grass, they saw a large circle in the shape of the one they had been sitting in.

Academic Buildings and Dormitories

Ballantine Hall and the Tenth Floor

Almost no IU student can get away from the school without having at least one course in Ballantine Hall, which has been given the "Suicide Tower" moniker on campus due to the repeated tragic accounts of people taking their lives here. This box-shaped building, which was, at one time, the largest academic building on a university campus anywhere in the world, was built in 1959 and holds classes of every sort. Not many know that the formula for fluoride was invented in this building, which means Indiana University reaps some royalties to this day.

Ballantine Hall. Once the largest academic building in the United States, it has ten floors and offers a multitude of different types of classes. *Courtesy of Lauren Clark, 2021.*

Students share in the bitterness of climbing the strangely difficult stairs in order to reach their classes. The stairs are so difficult to climb just to the second floor that even riders preparing for IU's annual cycle race, the Little 500, have been known to use this stairwell for training. Students get overly winded, struggling to make it, no matter how fit or healthy they are. All IU Hoosiers understand the immense pain and exhaustion from these stairs, which seem to be the most difficult steps to climb in one's life.

Students sometimes cheat the system by taking the elevator in the central lobby of the building to one of the upper floors and then walk down the stairs to the floor their class is on. The elevators don't go to the two floors everyone usually needs. The painfulness of climbing the stairwell isn't due to the stairwell and the building being haunted, however; it is due to the poor design of the building's architecture, as the space wasn't designed with efficient airflow needed to breathe. Due to the low supply of air, one must work harder to breathe and, thus, it makes it unnecessarily difficult to climb these stairs. Pair this with a shoulder-to-shoulder crowd of students leaving and arriving for their classes and it's suffocating, exhausting and, sometimes, infuriating.

Almost as frightening as these notorious stairs is the tenth floor, which is known to some as a paranormal hotspot. The reason the tenth floor is so special may be due to the suicides that have taken place over the years near this floor. It's amazing to think that thousands of students, faculty and staff walk through this building daily, completely unaware of the building's dark history. In 1970, one twenty-eight-year-old graduate student leapt from the eighth floor, and in August 1999, another man at the age of forty jumped from a window on the ninth floor. Again, in November 2000, a twenty-four-year-old student leaped to his death from an eighth-story window.

Sightings include floating orbs and a janitor who appears to be a real, solid person but vanishes when approached. Bright flashes of light have also been seen, and according to one scary account, the banging of classroom doors have been heard. One night, while alone in the building, a security officer was making his rounds when sometime between 9:00 and 10:00 at night, all of the doors down both sides of one of the halls abruptly started shaking loudly, as if people were desperate to get out.

The entrance to Ballantine Hall. *Courtesy of Lauren Clark, 2021.*

Startled and confused, the officer ran to one of the doors and opened it to find that the room was empty and silent. A few doors down, the officer found that one professor was still in his office. When the officer asked the professor if anyone else was around, the professor was very befuddled and explained to the officer that all of the other professors had already gone home and that he was the last one there. For the professor, it had been quiet all night.

Owen Hall and the Severed Arm

One of the more disturbing stories, even without the paranormal events, occurred in Owen Hall, which is one of the oldest buildings on campus. Originally, Owen Hall housed the School of Natural Sciences. Cadavers were often donated to the school to use in their classes, and a dumbwaiter was used to lift the bodies from the main floor to the upper floor to the classrooms. Because of the small size of the dumbwaiter, the limbs would often get stuck in the shaft, which would tear them off. It's said that instead of cleaning out the dumbwaiter, the limbs were left at the bottom, where they fell. Perhaps it's the spirits who donated their cadavers to the university who continue to have a connection to the body parts left at the bottom of the shaft that creates the cold spots and moving or vanishing objects.

However, the story gets more disturbing than torn, decaying limbs. A nursing student who was not liked by her peers due to her pretentious attitude was involved in a horrific prank gone morbidly wrong. Sometime in the mid-twentieth century, a group of students decided to play a nasty joke on the girl. The students took an arm from one of the cadavers and broke into the girl's dorm room. After tying the arm to one of the ceiling lights in her room, they fled outside and waited in the dark for the nursing student to arrive home.

They waited as they watched her eventually enter the dormitory, expecting to hear the girl's blood-curdling screams. They never came. After waiting for some time, the silence had become worrying to the group, so they made their way into the building and back to the dorm room. Instead of finding the student fainted, crying or running down the hallway, they found her door open, her sitting on the ground with the severed arm in her own, rocking herself and gnawing on it. No accounts explain what happened to the girl, but it's probably safe to say that the cruel incident drove her to insanity.

The entrance to Owen Hall. *Courtesy of Lauren Clark, 2021.*

Career Development Center and the Good Doctor

Hidden behind massive trees, located off Tenth Street and North Jordan Avenue, is an early twentieth century building with a grisly past. Across from the Herman B. Wells Main Library, this office, which was originally built as a home, has been haunted for decades by a mad doctor known as the "Good Doctor," a young girl and, possibly, babies who died in the building. The staff who works within the building seem to see the strangest happenings on the second floor, with the spiral staircase being the ghostly hotspot. The original owner of the home, whom people claimed built his home out of insanity, put a pistol against his head in the basement, ending his life.

Sometime in the 1950s, a doctor purchased the home and lived and worked in what is now known as the Career Development Center (CDC), treating people in the community and at Indiana University. At this time, because abortions were illegal, scared and helpless women, including those who attended the university, desperately sought the Good Doctor's help. The doctor performed illegal abortions in secrecy, and every night, after a day of operations, he would discard the unborn fetuses by incinerating them in the coal shoot. After the remains were cremated, he would hide them in the basement, under the floor, inside the walls and around the spiral staircase inside the home.

Unfortunately, the Good Doctor's fate would forever change when a young seventeen-year-old female came to him for a hushed abortion sometime during the early 1950s. During the young lady's operation, the doctor hit a major artery, and she bled to death on his operation table. In a panic, the doctor slid her lifeless body down the coal shoot, incinerated her, cleaned up the blood and hid the remains under the spiral staircase with the other remains of the unborn fetuses. Because the girl had a family she was close with, an investigation was conducted by authorities, who questioned the doctor. Suspecting him as either a kidnapper or murderer, the police arrested the man; however, as a doctor with enough money to make bail, he returned to his home on the campus.

Sometime after his return home, it's said that the frightened man carried a rope with him to the top landing of the spiral staircase, tied a noose around his neck and jumped to his death, his neck breaking instantly. It's not known how long it was before he was found, but his hanging body was found dangling above the steps when the authorities returned to his home to question him further about the girl's disappearance. There are no records or police reports of cremated remains being found at this location. Sadly, it seems that the Good

Front entrance of the 625 North Jordan Avenue, which was once the Career Development Center at Indiana University. *Courtesy of Lauren Clark, 2021.*

Doctor, the seventeen-year-old girl and, possibly, the souls of the fetuses have been trapped within the building all these years, according to the people who have encountered them in some way decades later.

Sometime after the doctor's suicide, Indiana University purchased and started leasing out the building to a fraternity, Phi Kappa Tau, which saw this as a positive opportunity, having lived in the old Buskirk-Showers Mansion that was farther from campus. The fraternity used this location as its home in the early 1970s, it's said. The very day that the first fraternity member, Danny J., moved in, the spirits made their presence known. As the young man was in his room, unpacking, he heard footsteps climbing down the spiral staircase. Thinking the sound belonged to one of his fraternity brothers, Danny exited his second-floor room and went looking for the person.

Although the young man searched and called out, no one responded, and there were no other beings in the building. As he stood in the middle of the staircase, obviously confused and looking around, he felt a cold hand place itself on his shoulder, which he stated felt like an icy mist. He turned around and looked behind him, but nothing was there. At that moment, the boy suffered from a seizure, and after his friends found him on the floor and took him immediately to the campus medical building, he explained what had happened.

Danny wasn't the only Phi Kappa Tau fraternity member to come in contact with a spirit, as another member had supposedly run right through a transparent man—again, on the second floor—and then witnessed the man hurry up the spiral staircase and vanish right before his eyes. In a twisted form of hazing, it has also been said that the Phi Kappa Tau fraternity had used the coal shoot during its ritualistic hazing, forcing their new pledges to sit inside the dark, cramped shoot with a lit candle and wait until the fraternity brothers let them free. It's rumored that the flame from the candle would grow over a foot tall before being snuffed out.

Although it may be fun to imagine that this is the work of the supernatural, given the fact that happened inside an old coal shoot, it's more likely the cause was residual coal inside the shoot. This wasn't the only tradition that the fraternity house kept, however, as one student would be given one of the second-floor bedrooms, which was so tiny that it was almost the size of closet. Not only was the room unwanted due to its size, but the room was rumored to be cursed; the student to whom the room belonged would either drop out or flunk out from the university. According to an *Indiana Daily Student* article from 1984, almost all of the residing fraternity brothers had experienced strange things around the time that the article was published. An interviewee admitted in the article to having heard unexplained noises: "There are noises. I've worked late before, and it can be a bit strange. One night, when I was working late—it was around a quarter after 12—I heard strange noises. It sounding like pounding. I left. My work was done anyway."

Since the old home is now used as university offices, the spirits of the deceased have been heard and seen, including the girl who died during her surgery. Like the doctor, she's always encountered on the second floor of the house. The Good Doctor's apparitions have also been seen climbing the spiral staircase or hanging from the landing, his ghostly figure swaying back and forth. Staff members and the fraternity brothers have claimed throughout the decades to have heard the sound of babies crying, especially late at night, which is a longtime favorite ghost story throughout the campus. Kitchen staff who have worked in the building always quit eventually, since the sound of infants crying and scratching from somewhere inside the walls disturbed and probably scared them. Others have claimed that the sound of infants crying can be heard even from outside the building.

IU Auditorium and the Blood Stain

The first building that former university president Herman B. Wells had erected was the grand IU Auditorium, with stunning architecture and constructed with none other than Indiana's own limestone. The IU Auditorium website boasts it is a "gathering place, hosting a diverse array of world-class artists, entertainers, musicians and lecturers in our 3,200-seat theatre." Not just for Indiana University attendees, the auditorium exists for the entire community and brings world-class entertainers, Broadway musicals, lecturers, comedians and musicians. *Les Miserables*, *Cats* and the Metropolitan Opera are only a few of the thousands of world-famous performances to take place on this stage. It was Herman B. Wells's vision for IU Bloomington to have the most famous music school in the world, as well as the Fine Arts Building, the Lilly Library and the IU Auditorium.

Since its opening on March 22, 1941, the IU Auditorium has also been used for special events, trade shows, ceremonies and weddings. Walking inside the main entryway through any of the multiple doors in the front of the building, look up and you'll see historically significant Thomas Hart Benton murals. The large paintings, which stretch horizontally near the ceiling, above the marble walls show Indiana's rich cultural and industrial history. Past the main entrance and through another set of double doors, you'll find yourself in a long, carpeted room with rich woods and orange-and-purple carpet. On the walls, there are elegant paintings and gold trim around the doors, and the room has leather sofas and benches for guests. Just like the architecture on the outside of the building, the inside is stunning.

Unfortunately, many times, people are injured and sometimes killed during the construction of large buildings. This 65,200-square-foot building is no different. In the early 1900s, airplanes were relatively new inventions and, thus, were not often seen daily. One construction worker, while high up on scaffolding above the stage, noticed an airplane flying overhead. Because the ceiling had not yet been completed, the interior of the auditorium was open to the elements and the sky overhead. The construction worker, distracted by the airplane, lost his balance on the scaffolding and fell to his death on the stage area below. The man didn't suffer, as the fall killed him immediately; however, the incident left a massive pool of blood around him.

The poor man's body and the bloody mess were cleaned up, and the construction of the auditorium was completed. It wasn't long after the building's completion that the pool of blood returned to the exact place where the man's death occurred. The staff did everything they could think of to clean up the blood stain, including scrubbing and bleaching, but it wouldn't budge. Finally, the ultimate fix was attempted by replacing the wooden floorboards stained with the blood. While this seemed to work for some time, the staff was horrified to see the exact same blood stain return to the new wooden floor. They replaced the wood not once, but twice, to resolve the problem, but no matter what they did, the blood would seep through to the new wood. Finally, in defeat, the staff covered the stain with a rug.

Rumors have swirled around the auditorium in relation to the worker's death. One myth is that the blood spot will show up again during a rainstorm or a particularly dramatic performance on the theater's stage. Janitors have supposedly turned the lights off at night, walked three feet or so away from the light switch, only to see the lights have come right back on. Actors and actresses performing in the auditorium have reported looking in the mirrors in their dressing rooms, shocked to observe someone standing right behind them, staring at their reflection. When they turn around to see the person standing behind them, no one is there.

On a separate occasion, one campus security officer watched as a man entered the auditorium. The building was closed to the public and locked up at this time, so the guard ran into the building to find him. As soon as the guard entered the building, he heard the intruder's footsteps and followed them through the building. The thudding sound of the man's feet hitting the ground led the security officer down corridors lined with closed and locked-up doors. Finally, the guard heard the guy walk into a room, which he entered. On looking at his surroundings, the guard realized that there was no one in the empty room but himself. It was at this moment that the guard stood there in the room, most likely very confused; he heard an evil cackle from outside of the room and in the hallway he had just run through. The guard rushed back out into the hallway and pointed his flashlight around. As expected, he was alone.

McNutt and the Hatchet Man Murder

Unfortunately, Indiana University is no stranger to murders on or near campus. One of the most terrifying tales takes place at the McNutt Residence Hall. Apparently, in 1998, a clairvoyant by the name of Jean Dixon predicted a dangerous man would escape from a mental institution and murder a female coed at one of the top-three universities in Indiana. The rumor is said to have created a panic throughout universities and those staying on campuses after it was reported in the media. The premonition was said to have been broadcast on the *Oprah Winfrey Show*, where it was stated that one of the Big Ten college campuses would be the setting for a madman who would be dressed in a costume from Little Bo Peep and would be carrying a hatchet, knife or other weapon. This rumor was disproven, as no such episode existed; it was only the creation of an elaborate scare, which is retold every now and then across university campuses. Nevertheless, a grisly murder did occur on campus by a Hatchet Man decades earlier. One year, around Thanksgiving break in the late 1960s, the City of Bloomington issued a state of warning, as there was a serial killer on the loose with a hatchet. The city advised all residents to remain indoors; this, unfortunately, didn't stop the murderer.

While most students travel back home for the holiday to be with relatives, two college girls had to stay on campus over the break. After only a few days, one of the girls was experiencing cabin fever and wanted to attend a party on campus. Although the party wasn't far from their dormitory, the girl's roommate reminded her of the citywide warning and urged her not

A sketch of McNutt Residence Hall. *Courtesy of Stephanie Huber of HUBERart.*

to attend the party and to stay home with her. Against the wishes of her roommate, she left the dorm and walked to the party alone in the dark. Immediately after her roommate left, the other girl locked the door behind her and settled down for a night alone.

During the evening, the girl heard a scratching at the door and grew frightened that the sound was being made from the hatchet murderer standing outside her door. As the scratching continued loudly, the scared student hid herself in the closet, while the scratching continued. Over the next half hour or so, the scratching at the door grew fainter and fainter until the noise finally ceased completely. The student who had hid herself in the closet, most likely to hide in case the murderer broke inside, fell asleep, curled up at the bottom of the closet floor.

She awoke when she heard a loud, heart-stopping pounding at the door. Scared again, she asked who was knocking at her door, and a police offer responded. When the girl opened the door for the police officer, the sight that welcomed her was an awful one. Two police officers were standing in front of a black body bag. The girl's roommate had, for some reason, turned around on her way to the party and headed back to her dorm room, probably to retrieve something she had forgotten.

When the girl had reached the dormitory, the hatchet murderer had struck the back of her skull with the weapon before fleeing into the night. The bleeding, wounded girl had not yet died but was able to crawl inside the building and all the way back to her dorm room. The scratching that her roommate had heard was the sound of the girl's final moments as she scratched on the door, attempting to get her roommate's attention. Other versions of the story state that the deceased girl's throat was slit and that her hands were worn down to the bone, due to her desperately clawing at the door.

The Hatchet Man Strikes Again

It's believed there were additional sightings of the notorious Hatchet Man, as there are multiple records and interviews within the Indiana University archives. Mary Temple noted one story from May 1961, in which a young couple wanted to park their car in a secluded part of town in order to have some alone time. Although one police officer stopped them on their way to a dark place to park their vehicle and warned them about a mad man on the loose, they continued anyway. While parked, the girl grew increasingly nervous regarding the hatchet man until, finally, the girl was able to convince her date to take her home.

On their drive back to the girl's home, a convertible car followed behind them, and with every turn or maneuver, the car continued to follow them. This went on for several miles until, after some time, the car pulled up next to the young man and woman with the window rolled down. The person in the other car was a man, who warned the two of them that the hatchet man was sitting on the roof of the car.

This urban legend is a very common one in the United States and the United Kingdom. Those who know Alvin Schwartz's *Scary Stories to Tell in the Dark* book series will probably remember one unsettling story in the first novel, *High Beams*. Hoosiers who are fans of *Scary Stories to Tell in the Dark* and *More Scary Stories to Tell in the Dark* will be pleased to know that Schwartz used multiple Hoosier folklore resources to inspire his stories. While this particular story was recorded by Mary Temple of Bloomington in May 1961, this tale may be a variation of the original account from Iowa, which tells the same story, only with one girl driving alone at night. On the other hand, it's quite possible this narrative is true, as the Hatchet Man did exist and terrorize the city of Bloomington in the 1960s. In 1970, a sixteen-year-old girl was interviewed about the incident:

> *There was this boy and girl out, oh, parked on Riverside Drive. They had an argument, and they both slid to their respective sides of the car, and just as they slid over, this hatchet came right through the convertible top of the car. There was a man on top of the car with a hatchet who intended to kill them both.*

Since there's no additional information about this variation of the story, one can't know for sure if this version of the Hatchet Man story is fact. The sixteen-year-old girl had heard this information from one of her high school peers, and that the incident had happened north of Indianapolis, in Upland, Indiana. Although the young lady was skeptical about the event, her schoolmate believed it; yet neither of them knew how the young couple in the car escaped.

As frightening as this story is and as difficult as it is to believe, it may not be myth at all, since another record from April 30, 1968, was reported by Les Freiberger during an interview of the event. This account retold the same story, with the added fate of the young couple and the hatchet man. Instead of Upland, Indiana, the attack happened south of Indianapolis in

Columbus, just east of Bloomington, and the young man and woman in the car were listening to the radio when a news report regarding the escaped convict came on the radio. The boy and girl were sitting very close to each other when a hatchet came right through the ceiling of the car. The couple, terrified and trying to escape their attacker, took the car out of park and sped away for safety. When the police were called out to the scene, they found the hatchet man lying on the ground, dead, having been run over by the boy's car.

Magee Hall, Foster Quadrangle

In the late 1990s, two male freshmen from Maryland shared room 13 in the Foster-Magee dormitory, which is now known as Magee Hall in the Foster Quadrangle. The excited young students loved attending Indiana University and were actively enjoying their first year at the university by making many friends, attending parties and even enjoying the courses they were taking. As Halloween approached, the boys' anticipation was growing, and they eagerly planned their costumes. After deciding between ghosts and goblins, they decided to attend the Halloween party on campus dressed as scary goblins.

The Friday night of the Halloween arrived, and the Foster-Magee Residency Hall was alive with the entire first floor of male students getting dressed to go out. Just as the two roommates in room 13, excited to finish dressing in their costumes and leave for the party early, were starting to apply their fake blood to their goblin costumes, the lights in the building went out and made everything pitch-black. On a normal day, a power outage is usually nothing more than that; however, as this was Halloween night, and the students living in the dormitory were either startled by this or were scared already. To their relief, the lights in the building came back on, and everyone was able to see again.

All of the male students on the first floor were finished dressing and began to leave for the party. Noticing their friends in room 13 had not come out of their room yet, their neighbors knocked on their door. After knocking numerous times, the door slowly opened on its own, and the students entered the two boys' dorm room, showing no one inside the room. Neither of the boys were found in the building, nor at the party. Search parties for the two young men were supposedly conducted for weeks after their disappearance. Neither ever turned up. The urban legend surrounding the Magee Hall

Residence Center is that every Halloween night, someone goes missing from the dormitory, especially if they are residences of room 13, as it's supposedly cursed. Of course, this is completely false, and searches online will bring up no record of two male Indiana University students having gone missing in this fashion.

Collins Living-Learning Center and Room 207

I ain't afraid of no ghosts.
—Ray Parker Jr.

It's one type of experience when one goes through an extraordinarily unexplained event; however, it's a different experience entirely when someone experiences the occurrence with others. This is what happened to three young coeds living in the Collins Dormitory in 2002. Collins, known among its students as "Hoosier Hogwarts," is a very large limestone building that resembles a castle much like the IMU does. Collins is divided into different groups, and each has its own medieval-style banner. The dining hall is very large, with high ceilings decorated in these banners.

Two boys, who we will refer to as "Adam" and "Jake," were roommates in room 207, and their friend "Eric," who has recounted the stories in this section, was staying down the hall in room 204. Adam and Jake would repeatedly tell their friend about the annoying, mysterious pounding that would come through the walls and on their door at night. Of course, the two young men believed the loud pounding at the door was merely the prank of another coed. The pounding noise that was coming through the wall was thought to be the pipes from the next door shared bathroom.

As time went on, the knocking and pounding noises grew louder and louder. The two roommates would often complain to their friend Eric about the sounds happening at night, as well as waking up in the middle of the night to find their bunk bed moved out and away from the wall. The first time this happened, one of the two roommates went knocking on Eric's door, waking him up and asking him to come look. Eric followed back to room 207 and could see that the bunk bed was, indeed, moved out just a little way from the wall. More than just being mysteriously moved away from the wall, the bed was shaking for no reason, Adam would complain. This, too, became worse over the span of late September to the end of December that same year.

Unlike the other ghost stories and urban legends in this book, in which noises and objects move on their own for no known cause, this ghost story has an extraordinary aspect: one-on-one interactions between inanimate objects and the living. Items that were lying on the floor in the dorm room were said to have flown across the room, hitting one of the boys in the back while they were turned around. One time, Eric, from down the hall in room 204, witnessed this happening to Adam. Some items would just go missing entirely.

One of the IU students, Adam, had a *Ghostbusters* action figure in his room, which only adds to the irony of this story. The toy was usually kept on either the desk or the dresser in the room. At one point, Jake and Eric thought it would be fun to play a harmless prank on Adam by placing the action figure under the sheets in Adam's bed for him to find and, hopefully, feel startled or scared. Unfortunately, the pranksters didn't receive the reaction they were hoping for, as Adam had not mentioned anything about finding the toy in his bed sheets either that night or the next morning.

At some point, one of the boys decided to ask Adam if he had found the toy. Adam said that he wasn't aware of what they were talking about, as he hadn't found the toy in his bed that night. The friends checked the bed and the sheets but found no trace of the toy. Adam then sat at the desk, his roommate Jake standing behind him, when Eric casually stated, "I wonder what happened to that thing." At that very moment, the *Ghostbusters* action figure fell out of thin air, somewhere from the ceiling, and dropped onto the desk, falling behind it and onto the ground. They left the toy there for a little while until, later, one of the students got on the floor to retrieve the toy from under the desk, but it was not there. They had found the little toy holding onto the radiator by its little plastic arms.

This wasn't the only interaction the three friends had with Adam's action figure. On a completely separate occasion, the toy, which had been sitting on top of the desk, moved onto the dresser when the three friends were out of the room. Clearly wanting to investigate with open minds, the three boys exited the room, locking the door behind them, and hung out in the lounge for about five minutes before unlocking the door and reentering the room. To their shock, the toy had moved. This didn't seem possible to them, as all three had been out of the room and with each other the entire time. There was also no way for anyone else to enter the room.

Deciding to continue their experiment, they exited again, locked the door, waited for some time and then came back inside after unlocking the door. This time, the action figure hadn't moved locations, but it was in a completely difference stance than it had been before they left the room. Adam, Jake and Eric continued to perform this experiment by leaving the dorm room, waiting and coming back in, making sure to close and lock the door. Each and every time, the little action figure would be in a different stance.

At one point, the boys reentered the room, and the arm was torn completely off and missing. Perhaps whatever was causing this to happen was getting tired of the game. Not able to find the arm, or perhaps they didn't care to look for the arm at this point, the boys turned to leave the room once again. However, Adam was hit in the back by an object and turned around and looked down to see what had been thrown at him. It was the arm. The last time the three friends ran this test, they came back to find the figure's face had been completely melted away, as if someone had held a match or lighter up to it. Adam and Jake attested to the fact that there were no lighters or matches anywhere in their room. One of them had found that same faceless toy sitting on the sink in the bathroom that night.

As if this incident wasn't enough to put the boys on edge and make for an interesting ghost story, another unsettling interaction took place within Adam and Jake's room. Jake had a computer program that would speak in a computerized voice whenever it was on. In order to make the program speak, one only needed to type into the program, and the voice would repeat back what you were typing as you were typing it. What he didn't count on was the thing talking back to him and his friends. Even when no one was typing on the computer, the program would speak directly to the boys in the room.

The boys got to the point where they would ask the computer questions, only to have it answer back. When one of them was singing in the room, the program would comment, "I love that song." The program even knew who the boys were, since it called out the full first, middle and last names of one of the students. In their amazement, one of the friends got out a camera to capture the talking program on video. As expected, the program stopped talking completely, not answering any questions the boys asked and making no comments on what was being said or done within the room. When they turned off the camera, almost immediately, the program stated, "I'm camera shy."

Being intelligent boys, they figured this had to be the work of a computer hacker. If so, the hacker would be able to see and hear what was going on inside the room. However, the program was turned off and disconnected from the internet and the network when this happened. The three of them investigated the computer and the program, yet they found nothing suspicious. The computer continued to make comments and speak to the boys in the room for a couple of weeks afterward until it finally stopped. If this was the work of some ghost bound to room 207 in the Collins Dormitory, it eventually got bored of the joke. Either way, the three friends, who were clearly put off and scared by what had happened that one night with the camera, made the decision to not discuss the event again.

Over the next month or so, poor Adam couldn't take the disturbances any longer. He had stopped sleeping in his own bed in room 207 completely, spending every night in the lounge instead. Although he refused to sleep in the room, the young man was sure that whatever was haunting the dorm room had followed him to the lounge. The pounding on the walls and the door, as well as the other mysteries that had already been occurring had yet to cease, and the boy wasn't getting any sleep at night.

Jake continued to sleep in room 207 in the bottom bunk bed, where he had always slept. When people in Collins asked Jake about the hauntings, he would either dismiss it or laugh it off. This doesn't mean that the phenomena wasn't happening while he continued to sleep alone in that room. The same things that had happened before continued, but Jake ignored it all and pretended that none of what was happening was real.

When Eric went to visit Jake in room 207 one night, Eric retold the story of how there was a knocking from the inside of the door as he approached the door from the outside. Eric knocked back on the door, only to receive more knocking from the other side. Eric knocked. It knocked again. Finally, Eric continuously knocked until a sleepy Jake answered the door, having been asleep with the lights off. As Jake turned on the light after answering the door for his friend, Eric peered around Jake, and they both saw Jake's bed sheet move off of the bed and hang horizontally, outstretched across the room in midair. Jake ran across the room and tore down the bed sheet. As he did, a desk drawer that had already been opened slammed shut forcefully.

Around this time, Adam just couldn't take it anymore. He applied to move to another dormitory on campus and was approved, allowing him to move into a completely different residence somewhere else on campus the following semester. Jake later left Collins and ended up living somewhere off IU's campus. Eric, on the other hand, continued to reside in the same room, 204, for either three more years or a total of three years. After Adam and Jake moved out of their shared room, no further disturbances happened to Eric or anyone else living in room 207 over those three years.

Teter Dormitory and the Laughing Laundry Room

Joining in the other dormitory ghost tales, the Teter Residence Hall has its fair share of things that go bump in the night. Students sound asleep in their beds or studying for their classes have been startled by loud bangs. The banging noise has been described as an aggressive knocking on a door, which is often heard near the boiler room. While students have attempted to investigate the origin of the sounds, they have found nothing. The buildings all around campus are quite old; therefore, it is probable that the loud banging they're hearing is from the boiler room, the plumbing or the air conditioning. However, IU Bloomington does well to make sure everything is up to code and is in working order.

Still, this doesn't explain the reason why the student residents of Teter haven't liked doing their laundry. If you believed college students don't enjoy doing laundry in a normal setting, know that this is even truer considering the building's laundry room is haunted by a laughing spirit. Perhaps this has been a wild excuse the students have used in order to put off washing their clothing and bedding; however, coeds have sworn there is a ghost causing the banging noises—and it's not coming from the washers and dryers.

Students have heard the sound of a bag moving around when they were completely alone in the room, as well as the sound of laughing, similar to the sound of a child's laugh. Clearly not a malevolent spirit, the laughing ghost has been said to play tricks on those doing their laundry by turning the sink faucets in the laundry room on and off. Students have either seen or heard the water running when the faucet was turned off, only to witness the water shutting itself off and then back on again. Friendly or not, students don't enjoy going to the basement alone to do their laundry, so many either don't go at night, or they take a buddy with them.

Read Hall and the Girl in Yellow

Read Hall, which sits between the Musical Arts Center and Jacobs School of Music, was named after Professor Daniel Read, one of the earlier professors at the university. The residence hall houses male and female students in opposite wings, as the building is in a distinct X shape. Unfortunately, while numerous deaths have taken place at the Read Hall on Third Street, one in particular sticks in the mind of students and faculty who've heard the story. There are multiple variations of the origins to the legend of the ghost girl with long hair in the yellow dress, but the ending appears to be the same across the board of storytellers.

Oddly enough, the haunts were only reported in the 1960s, when one particularly ghastly murder happened between two university students in the late 1950s or early 1960s. As the legend goes, a premedical student and his beautiful seventeen-year-old girlfriend had an ugly argument, which was a common occurrence between the two. Unfortunately, this argument was their last, as it had a deadly ending. The argument supposedly started at a party where the girl was wearing a yellow dress, but the couple returned back to the privacy of the boyfriend's third-floor dorm room. The couple continued to argue, either over jealousy or a breakup, when the boyfriend ended the fight by taking one of his scalpels and murdering his girlfriend by slitting her throat and exposing her trachea. One variation of the legend argues that the male student didn't just slit his girlfriend's throat but cut off her face and hid it inside one of his dresser drawers.

However, the premedical student wasn't finished, as he supposedly put the young girl's body, in her yellow party dress, in the boiler room, although others claim he hid her in the tunnel underneath the residence hall, next to the laundry room. It is a known fact that there is an extensive underground tunnel system that branches out under multiple buildings and different parts of the campus. These tunnels, which are extremely dangerous and closed off to everyone, are used for ethernet cables, electrical wiring and the like. The interesting fact about the tunnels is that, while some are so small that only steam can pass, other areas are large enough for a person to walk through. The murderer was said to have gone directly to jail, immediately following the crime; however, other accounts state he was admitted into a mental asylum in Indianapolis. Either way, the seventeen-year-old student was buried, and the strange phenomenon and sightings started occurring sometime afterward.

The apparition of a girl in a bloody yellow dress has been spotted by students and residence assistants (RAs) living at the Read Center, always without her face. These reported apparitions are almost always the same: a young girl in a yellow dress, covered in blood, with her long black hair hiding her face as she floats down the hallways or lurks in dorm rooms or the laundry areas. Electrical issues have also happened from time to time, with stereos spiking loudly and randomly by themselves, usually on the third floor—the same floor where the girl's life was taken.

In the summer of 2002, one of the RAs saw the apparition. Standing where several hallways connect in the shape of an X, the doors started

The infamous Girl in Yellow has been seen multiple times, covered in blood at the Read Residency Hall. *Courtesy of Lauren Clark, 2021.*

opening and slamming shut on their own. In the RA's peripheral vision, she saw a yellow dress. Instead of finishing the task of updating the hallway bulletin board, the RA quickly left in fear. Doors in the dorm rooms have also been known to slam shut at random times, day and night, for no reason at all. Sometimes, this happens in the wee hours of the morning.

Probably one of the most terrifying accounts of Read Hall residents experiencing an encounter with the girl in yellow was reported in the 1970s, when a male student was working on his studies alone in his dorm room. Out of nowhere, a cold chill filled the room, and the boy turned around in his chair to find the cause of the sudden iciness—he found himself face-to-face with the girl in all her gory horror, with only a gaping hole where her face should be. She had been floating behind him, watching him silently while he studied. The very moment he whirled around in his seat and saw her, she dissipated into a mist, and the student's room became warm again, leaving him alone. Some have seen her lurking near the laundry room where her body was discovered or traveling the floor, perhaps in search for her lost face.

Another death resulting in a separate legend stems from the incident in which a woman named Paula committed suicide on a December day the winter before the student was due to graduate from Indiana University. As the story goes, the student, an overworked resident assistant, learned that her grades had dropped, jumped from the sixth-floor stairs and broke her neck. Students living in the Read Center have reported doors inside the dorm rooms slamming shut day and night, for no reason at all. In the summer months, when it's very hot inside the building, the students will feel sudden cold spots that will quickly become warm again. Being university students, it's likely they knew well enough that the air conditioning wasn't on at these times. Students living in Read Hall have also reported hearing screams every December 12, the anniversary of the girl's death. The screams, of course, come from the building's stairwell.

Greek Ghosts

Alpha Phi Sorority and the Cold Room

Some of the sororities and fraternities on campus are housed in some of the oldest buildings on IU's property, since they were once houses long ago. The Alpha Phi Sorority was once the home of a distinguished IU professor, who resided in the home with his only child, a young daughter. The father and daughter were very close, and when the young girl died from polio, the man was distraught. Other rumors will tell you that, instead of polio, the daughter became insane and hanged herself in her bedroom. In any case, the father was devastated over the loss of his daughter. While it seems some who have heard the ghost story don't know whether he passed away in the home or moved out, one source claims that he moved out of the home. Either way, Indiana University eventually ended up buying the old house, which became the home of the Alpha Beta chapter of Alpha Phi, one of the first Greek societies for women.

Around early 2000s, some of the sorority sisters began to report that they were seeing the spirit of the little girl and her father in the cold rooms in the building. If you've never heard of a cold room, you're not alone. Cold rooms are a common sleeping area where it is very dark and the temperature is kept very low. Numerous beds line the inside of the cold room, and students will sleep there to get a restful night's sleep, as sleeping in cooler temperatures is better for your body.

Alpha Phi Sorority at IU. *Courtesy of Stephanie Huber of HUBERart.*

Inside the smaller cold room in the old house, the legend goes that, every four years, the spirit of the professor's daughter will allow herself to be seen; she's redheaded and wearing a white nightgown while walking around the room. This could be, of course, the recollection of someone's nightmare. It's said that, in order for this to happen, someone must wake up in the middle of the night at just the right time.

Others rumors state that the professor himself has been seen wearing a trench coat in one of the other rooms in the house, where he could have spent most of his time during his life. Rooms 12 and 13 are also said to have belonged to the professor's only child, and they are believed to have been where she died. During one of the ceremonies held at the sorority's house, one of the sisters left something in her room upstairs and went to fetch it. As she was on her way to her room, all of the upstairs lights were off, and there stood the man in the trench coat. She went to her room, and convinced that this man was real, she dialed the police. Although the authorities searched the entire house, the man was never found.

Kappa Delta Rho, and the Nightmare in Room 104

One urban legend surrounding the Kappa Delta Rho fraternity is an old one that may not have been spoken in a decade or two. We know that a young man who was a member of the fraternity didn't survive a car accident around the late 1950s or early 1960s. As the story goes, finals week was over at Indiana University, and the students were finally able to relax and have some fun. Some students went home to be with their families during the school break, while others chose to stay behind on and off campus.

For the fraternity of Kappa Delta Rho, the majority of the brothers had left to return home, aside from the house manager and his girlfriend. Hoping to have some alone time with each other after finals, the house manager and his girlfriend retired to his room, 104. Unfortunately for the two lovers, the house manager was called away on an emergency, leaving his girlfriend to wait for him in his room.

According to the legend that was told in the early 1990s, the girlfriend waited in the room for her boyfriend to return. As she began to feel cold and lonely, she wrapped her arms around her and drifted off to sleep. It was at this point that the young woman had a very disturbing nightmare. While still in the room, dead, gnarling branches from the tree outside the window crept into the room and stretched out around her, frightening her.

While she was trapped inside the cold, dark room, she could feel she was not alone. Sensing she was being watched from behind, the girl slowly turned around to find that a dark, towering figure was in there with her, watching her from the shadows. The looming figure moved toward her, bringing itself out of the darkness and into the little light that was coming from somewhere inside the room—possibly the moonlight.

When the girl saw the creature, she was horrified to find what looked like a man, but he was mangled beyond recognition. The man was covered in blood, and his flesh was torn from his body, hanging off him. In his bloody appearance, the student could see his tendons, twisted around each other and dangling from his body, with a pickax in one hand, which gleamed in the moonlight. She was frozen by the sight of him, so she couldn't run or even scream. The girl ran—to where, we aren't sure. Yet, at a certain part in her nightmare, she heard the sound of the pickax cutting through the air in her direction.

Finally, she realized that, in order to escape the killer, all she needed to do was to wake herself up, which she did. The fraternity brothers who were still staying at the house over the break heard the scream of a frightened girl coming from room 104. The young men rushed into the room to find the house manager's frightened girlfriend. We can assume the girl explained her nightmare, and all seemed to be okay in the end. Nevertheless, there was one thing the boys noticed that didn't add up. In the corner of the room, they found a pickax propped up against the wall.

As expected, there are many theories, beliefs and skepticism involving this unusual urban legend. Many people believe that the entire story was the work of a very scary nightmare and nothing more. A few students who have told this story in the past have believed the man with the pickax was the young fraternity member who was killed in the automobile accident, thus explaining the madman's torn skin and exposed tendons. Perhaps this ordeal was a joke played on the girl by other students, or perhaps it never happened at all but was created as a scary story to tell to the other fraternity members.

Poor Michael

IU student dies after cannon mishap

INDIANAPOLIS (U P I) — Michael Pfrang, 20, an Indiana University sophomore, had been sharing the excitement Saturday of homecoming parade festivities in Bloomington when he set a torch to a cannon.

Twelve hours later he was pronounced dead at Indianapolis Robert Long Hospital.

The cannon exploded at its base, hurling Pfrang into the street as the crowd watched horrified. The Petersburg IU student, only moments before, had been riding a Sigma Phi Epsilon float designed as a pirate ship.

He was the son of Mr. and Mrs. James Smith, Petersburg.

Spokesmen at the hospital said Pfrang's death resulted from severe head injuries.

News clipping "IU Student Dies After Cannon Mishap." *Courtesy of the* Daily Journal *of Franklin, Indiana, October 22, 1968.*

The story of "Poor Michael" is another old legend that's been around for decades and comes in multiple variations. The story begins sometime in the 1930s, when IU Bloomington was having its annual homecoming carnival. The parade theme was "Gun Down the Hawks of Iowa." Sticking to the theme of the event, one of the parade floats was expected to wow the onlookers by having a cannon in place to shoot confetti and streamers out of it. I'm sure, dear reader, you can already see where this story is heading. Unfortunately, a young fraternity pledge was tragically killed when the cannon backfired, and, instead of only shooting confetti and streamers, shrapnel flew out at the poor student, killing him instantly. However, Michael's soul apparently continued to linger. Members of his fraternity (there's no direct record of which one) claimed to hear footsteps and the sound of scrubbing in their house.

Before Michael died, like many new pledges, it was his duty to clean the bathroom in the basement. Although the fraternity denied it later, the *Indiana Daily Student* article from 1911, which is kept in the IU archives, notes on the fraternity brothers hearing Michael whistling away in the basement restroom, along with the distinct sound of him scrubbing. Items had also been found falling off shelves for no apparent reason, and one person in the fraternity house even saw the apparition of Michael in the basement. It seems that poor Michael continues to carry out his pledge duties, even in his afterlife—perhaps not even aware he's passed.

Zeta Beta Tau

The very northern part of IU Bloomington's campus is where many of the large fraternity and sorority houses stand. One in particular, at 1550 North Jordan Avenue, is a very nice-looking building with red brick halfway up the walls and smooth beige siding up to the roof. The three-story fraternity has a small, semicircular glass atrium at the front and center part of its first floor. A beautifully kept green lawn extends all the way to Jordan Avenue, and a long sidewalk, sometimes decorated nicely with sidewalk chalk promoting events like the Little 500, runs all the way to the glass doors.

The house has an unfortunate history, as public record will recollect about the arson fire from the 1980s, which burned the building beyond repair. One fraternity brother perished in the blaze, and the person who started the fire after becoming mentally impaired by alcohol, was sentenced to prison time. Supposedly, the cornerstone on which the Richmond student died was kept (probably in his honor) and used to build the new building.

Although the Zeta Beta Tau fraternity was rebuilt beautifully, it's rumored that the house is inhabited by the ghost of the young man from Richmond who died. Sometime after the fire, it was reported that the occupants were complaining about many disturbances in the bedrooms, kitchen and formal area of the building. At first, a mezuzah, a scroll affixed to the doorposts of Jewish homes, was placed inside the home in hopes of remedying the issues. The mezuzah is usually housed in a casing and either nailed, glued or screwed onto the right side of the door, positioned vertically. It's believed to provide protection to those inside the home, as well serve as a reminder that our homes are holy places and should be treated as such. After a while, with the bothersome occurrences inside the home continuing, the mezuzah was moved to one of the outside doorposts.

According to an interview kept in the IU archives, sometime in the early 2000s, a student was walking home from one of the libraries on campus, when they got back to the building and settled in for the night, watching television in the formal room. Realizing they were hungry and needed a snack, the fraternity member got up and went into the kitchen for a Pop-Tart. The TV apparently kept attempting to shut itself off, and when the student finally walked back in, shut the television off and left for the living quarters, the blinds behind him started to fly around for no reason. As the student moved down the hall, the blinds on the windows followed him, flying around from side to side until he reached his room. In another interview, someone who was relaxing in the living space of the house noticed the lights flicker on and off.

Office Buildings

The Old Millen House

Probably one of the oldest homes in the city of Bloomington has changed many hands and gone through many name changes since it was first built by the Millen family in 1845. It's a beautifully preserved 3,270-square-foot Presbyterian farmhouse with six bedrooms, one and a half baths and chimneys on opposite ends. William Millen built his farm on around 160 acres and constructed his Georgian-style home in a classical portico design, using bricks that he dug and fired on site and virgin walnut timber for the exterior. There is one central entrance with white columns on a raised square porch, and there are five windows spanning the front of the home. The interior is preserved as well, with antique furnishings, yellow poplar floors, the original brick walls and walnut woodwork.

Over the past nearly two hundred years, the house has been a private home for other families and has held offices. Other names the Millen House has had are "Wellswood House," "Stallknect House" and, now, the "Raintree House," although historians and others still refer to the home as the "Millen House." The name for the "Raintree House" came from the two raintrees that sit on the property. In 1969, the university purchased the home, and the IU chancellor made an agreement with Thomas D. Clark, the former Organization of American Historians (OAH) executive secretary and IU history professor, to use the building as the national headquarters of the OAH, which it has since 1970. On September 29, 2004, it was approved by the National Register of Historic Places as a historical site.

As it seems with buildings that are centuries old, years' worth of reports have been collected and published regarding strange events experienced by those working in the Raintree House. For those who work there on a daily basis, the sweet aroma of roses can be smelled when there aren't any around, and unrecognizable shapes moving just out of one's peripheral vision have been experienced, including the spirit of a woman who still lingers in the home.

In the 1850s, a washerwoman worked in the basement, cleaning the laundry in a vat of lye soap and, although it's found in many common household cleaners today, lye, a corrosive alkali that can be destructive and extremely toxic. Even a minuscule amount can cause third-degree burns in the mouth, esophagus and stomach and cause death. Due to this fact, lye has been used for murders and the disintegration of corpses throughout history. Tragically, the washerwoman of Raintree House had tripped and fallen into the vat of lye, killing her instantly.

According to many paranormal experts, dramatic and horrible events in history can sometimes leave a "residue," which can be experienced in a number of ways throughout time by the living. The Indiana Ghost Trackers

Pathway through Indiana University. *Courtesy of Zhen Li Photography.*

from Terre Haute visited the Raintree or Millen House in 2008. While the group was in one of the empty, uninhabited rooms, their electronic equipment picked up an unidentifiable voice whispering, "Basement… basement door."

Folklore Institute

In 1957, a famous folklorist and empire builder by the name of Richard Dorson came to Bloomington to establish the folklore department at the university. Previously, the sector was called the Folklore Institute and was located on 504 North Fess Street. The old two-story home has a deep redbrick exterior with white trim and a steeply angled roof with gray shingles. A very tall chimney is positioned at the front and center of the home and extends all the way past the second floor and the attic.

Two small windows in the shape of a fourth of a circle are visible on either side of the narrow chimney, giving the front of the house the appearance of having a human face. In the front part of the house, white columns create an awning on the first floor. To the left side of the front is a lovely blue-gray door with a rounded top and a circular window at the top of the door. Although the home is attractive and well-maintained, the structure does have a certain creepiness, most likely due to the face-like construction.

Richard Dorson worked tirelessly as the chair and director of the Folklore Institute, renaming the department the Department of Folklore and Ethnomusicology, and the sector was relocated to its current address, 802 East Third Street. According to those faculty, students and interns who worked in the building's offices, Dorson practically lived in his second-floor office. Sadly, the division lost its beloved director and chair in 1981, when he entered a coma after experiencing a heart attack while playing tennis. Dorson never came out of that coma.

It didn't take very long after his passing for those working in the office building or walking past it on the street to notice unusual events. Lights inside the building would flicker on and off, the sink faucets would be found running when people entered the home in the morning and a dim light or the shape of a male figure would be seen through the director's second-floor office window. One IU student was certain she saw Dorson standing in the window, looking out at her as she walked past on the sidewalk.

Even years after his passing, in the fall of 1981, a graduate student who was working inside the building happened to look outside the window when

504 North Fess Street, previously IU's Folklore Institute. *Courtesy of Nyttend.*

she exclaimed, "THAT'S DORSON!" Because he had such a distinct way of walking in his life, the girl was certain she was seeing Dorson walking, hunched over, with his face looking downward and carrying his papers. The student looked on as the man walked between the buildings at 504 and 506 North Fess Avenue. One account states that the student looked to the person she was with and looked back to see the mysterious man had vanished. Another slight variation is that she ran out of 504 North Fess Avenue after Dorson. When she hurried out to the space between the two buildings, the man was no longer in sight, and there was no one else around. It's said the grad student was quite shaken afterward.

Possibly the most interesting story, which folklore faculty and students swear happened, involves the old lamp. Attached to the exterior of the building, near one of the doors, was an old light that would stay on all night until the morning, when people arrived at the office. Every day, for years, that light would be on until it would automatically shut off around 8:00 in the morning, so faculty and students simply assumed that the outdoor light was set on a timer. However, out of the blue, the light started flickering until it finally shut off. Either a faculty member or student was coming into the house one morning, before 8:00 a.m., and the light was still off, making it very hard for them to see in the dark. Believing that perhaps the light just needed to be replaced or the wiring had gone bad, the grounds people called the electricians to come out and fix the light.

What the Folklore and Ethnomusicology Department didn't expect to hear was that there was no way this light should have been turning on to begin with, since it wasn't connected to anything to allow it to turn on. The department explained to the electricians that the light had been working properly for the past several years. Alarmingly, the electricians explained further that the light couldn't possibly have worked, because it had been disconnected for many years. No one was able to explain the incident, and the Folklore Department still feels complete confusion to this day.

2
Downtown Bloomington

At the very heart of downtown Bloomington, the courthouse sits in the middle of the square. The courthouse, which was completed in 1826, has a limestone exterior, a copper dome and a copper weathervane in the shape of a fish. When the courthouse was renovated in 1908, a remaining piece from the original building was used for the dome.

Four roads exist on all four sides of the courthouse, and shops, bakeries and restaurants line the four streets. Running east to west is Kirkwood Avenue, named after the 1895 astronomer Daniel Kirkwood, with the long street stretching all the way to the Sample Gates at the entrance of Indiana University. Along Kirkwood, one can find the 1920s-built Buskirk Chumley Theater, where Hoagy Carmichael used to play prior to his move to Hollywood. Plenty of restaurants, bars and shops line the street, some of which remain in the original buildings and houses from that time period. Campus stores, clothing retail stores and coffee shops appeal to the university students, who are often found shopping or sitting in front of them, their laptops and piles of books towering over them.

Parallel to Kirkwood Avenue, Fourth Street is known as the ethnic food hotspot of Bloomington, with lovely little homes lining both sides of the street, each of which offer a different type of cuisine. Thanks to Indiana University drawing people from all over the world to study, "Restaurant Row" features restaurants that serve Turkish, Tibetan, Thai, Japanese, Greek, Italian and more types of food. When stating that the food found on

Downtown Bloomington, Indiana. *Courtesy of White Iron Images.*

Fourth Street is 100 percent authentic, that is, by no means, putting it lightly. Each restaurant features meals cooked using the same preparation method you would find in the country of its origin.

On weekend nights, Kirkwood Avenue and the square are alive with music and students, who frequent the local bars. Kilroy's Sports, Kilroy's on Kirkwood and Nick's English Hut are just a few of the bars that have been around for decades, and it is a known college tradition to attend with friends. South Indiana Avenue intersects Kirkwood Avenue and also has plenty of local eateries and shops, a busy Starbucks and, according to a legend that dates back to the mid-1900s, one lingering ghost.

The Lady in Black Returns

Sighted many times stalking and prowling outside the Sample Gates, the lady in black is said to be the same spirit from Dunn Cemetery inside Indiana University's campus. While in the cemetery, she's seen sweeping across the graves; her behavior downtown is a little creepier. Usually seen in Victorian attire, with a long black dress and sometimes with a parasol, she has been

Downtown Bloomington, Indiana. *Courtesy of Jordanlhamann.*

sighted mostly near the corner of East Fourth Street and Indiana Avenue, which is just down the street from the Sample Gates.

The infamous ghost mysteriously mutters under her breath and often follows people at a distance as they walk past the little shops and restaurants, sometimes for a few blocks. Although there have been many accounts of her stalking people down the sidewalk, it's been stated that, when approached, she vanishes. Many university students have tried to catch the phantom, chasing her down the street, into alleyways or around corners before she mysteriously disappears or glides behind a tree.

Besides the very rare report of people throwing baseballs or stones in the apparition's direction, people leave the harmless lady in black alone. There are several logical explanations for this lingering lady, but none of them truly check out. One includes the lady as being a widow or mentally handicapped person who chooses to follow others, which doesn't explain how she vanishes when stones or other objects are thrown at her or when she is chased around the corner of a building, even though there are no nearby hiding spots where she could be.

Ghost Legs

Perhaps one of the more humorous stories to come from the paranormal experiences of downtown Bloomington include ghost legs or ghost pants. One Indiana University student made it known that as he was walking down the sidewalk on Third Street, a pair of legs wearing pants was walking in the opposite direction on the other side of the street. The fourth-year student, who made this incident known in 2006, claimed the legs were simply walking casually in a pair of faded blue jeans. While this is certainly the oddest story to come out of the haunting reports in the city, the reason could entirely be associated with the fact that the student saw the ghost legs late at night or early in the morning, when many downtown bars are open and frequented by IU students.

Monroe County History Center

202 East Sixth Street
Bloomington, IN 47408

According to Megan, the research librarian at the Monroe County History Center (MCHC), the center receives an average of five to six calls per year regarding haunts taking place in residents' homes or workplaces. Some callers inquire if the history center is haunted; however, the majority of callers

Monroe County History Center Collection. *Courtesy of EQRoy, April 11, 2018.*

are seeking advice or explanations for the unexpected occurrences they're experiencing in their own homes, which could be expected, as Bloomington is full of centuries-old homes. "Sometimes, someone is renting a house, and the landlord said something," Megan explained. People seem to always be looking for records of a murder, but rarely does anything come up.

Megan expressed that she's known "smart, sane, rational people who have seen some things" inside the MCHC. It appears that past events typically took place around employees of the building. In 2017, Megan started working in the building and was told the place was haunted. While walking down one of the hallways by herself, she heard the sound of rustling papers. She spun around, but no people, papers or even a slight breeze were seen or felt. She didn't think much of the incident and went about her business. Later, Megan brought the matter up to her coworkers and learned that she wasn't alone in experiencing strange happenings.

Ghost hunters have previously visited the old building and held séances, bringing with them an arrangement of electrical paranormal research equipment. One of the ghost hunters claimed to see a dog run down the block; however, instead of running down the street or sidewalk, it ran right through the buildings, as if they weren't there. The ghost tracking team set up their equipment inside the history center and heard a few weird sounds, and something supposedly moved. By the time they had finished conducting their research, they claimed there was energy in certain parts of the building.

Since the research librarian first started working at the MCHC, she recalls the cleaning staff refusing to enter the archives out of fear. The archives are kept in a closet-sized room in the basement, where there are no windows. It gives off a creepy, haunted appearance. In the basement with the archives are the old bathrooms that were once used when the building was the library, but the cleaning crew refused to clean the bathrooms down there after a startling event happened during one of their shifts. While cleaning at night, the double doors that opened up into one of the rooms flew open by themselves, as if a powerful gust of wind had blown them open. As the room is in the basement, where there are no windows and no wind could be felt, the staff stopped going down there to clean.

IRISH LION PUB AND RESTAURANT

212 West Kirkwood Avenue
Bloomington, IN 47404
www.irishlion.com

The most enjoyable pub in Bloomington is in a historic two-story brick building in the downtown square area. It's the Irish Lion Pub and Restaurant and is probably the most haunted pub in the entire state of Indiana. Rich in history, the original building was built in the late 1800s and has the most delicious food and drinks in the city. Just down one of the side streets, near the center of the downtown square, where the courthouse stands, it's a popular spot for families, university students and visitors.

On the east exterior wall of the brick building with cast iron columns is a weathered mural that once depicted a tobacco mail pouch with the words "Lovel Burch Hotel Bundy European," since tobacco was once sold here. The beautifully crafted wooden double doors at the very center of the pub's downstairs area, along with the woodwork, is original to the building, which was built in 1882. Although the stained glass in the exterior windows isn't from the original building, it was still created in the 1800s and brought down from Indianapolis.

The interior of the building was originally eighty feet long with a fifty-three-foot-long courtyard, which is now bricked in and used as a kitchen.

The front exterior of the Irish Lion Pub and Restaurant. *Courtesy of the Irish Lion, 2021.*

There are two floors: the downstairs pub and an upstairs eating area, which has a much larger seating area and is perfect for larger parties, families and events. The building was originally built as the Worley Tavern downstairs, and the Hotel Bundy European was located upstairs. The pub, today, boasts an impressive premier malt scotch whiskey selection numbering over two hundred, a full bar and a full menu of traditional Irish fare, steaks, stews, pub food and seafood.

The downstairs bar is split into two sections down the middle—the back bar and the front bar. The "back bar" in the main pub is a gorgeous mahogany bar that was built by Brunswick, the same manufacturer who makes billiards tables. The style of the bar, which is reminiscent of a Victorian pub in the Old World, was made between the late 1860s to the 1880s, and only three others are known to exist—in Paso Robles, California; Brookings, South Dakota; and downtown Denver, Colorado. The original back bar was originally located in a pub in Indianapolis before being relocated to the Irish Lion in Bloomington.

Overhead, in the downstairs area, a large collection of wooden ships hangs from the ceiling, and an even more impressive collection of taxidermy animals hangs on the walls above the bar and booths, giving the room an atmosphere similar to a pub in Ireland. The animals, which include foxes, moose, elk, pheasants and more were purchased at an auction from the Schmalz's Department Store Museum, which went out of business.

When the building was first built in 1882 by Zimri McCollough, an early settler and successful businessman who was active in the community and esteemed among his associates, the vision was to make the business a hotel (upstairs) and a pub (downstairs) in order to cater to and house the passengers of the Monon Train Depot that was across the street at the time. It was a very successful business. At the time, there was no gas, water or electricity in Bloomington, and kerosene gas lanterns hung from the ceiling in the downstairs pub. Decorative metal ceilings were installed in a diamond pattern as an aesthetically pleasing fire barrier from the gas lamps.

If one goes up the stairs to the left of the bar, they can tell without much effort that the purpose of the upstairs area was different than that of the main floor. At the top of the landing, there is a distinctive walkway that leads to the back of the building, where the vintage restrooms are. This served as the hotel's hallway, with the rooms off to the right side. Look up to the ceiling, and the wood molding from where the wall once stood can still be seen there and can give you an idea of how narrow the hall was and how big the hotel rooms were. Central heating didn't exist during this time, so each of the hotel rooms had one wood-burning stove. The wooden bar in the back of the main room is made of oak from 1910 from Rushville, Indiana.

The very front room of the upstairs area used to be the "House Madam" room, since the hotel did more than house weary travelers; the hotel also offered companions for the night. The Irish Lion's restaurant, which states on its website, "Sorry, this service is no longer available," now calls this room the Celtic Room. It is a beautifully Victorian-like room, with old, hand-painted portraits and large wooden sliding doors once used for privacy.

Over the course of the next one hundred years, the business offered a tavern, tobacco products, lunch and a game of pool. Unfortunately, Prohibition changed the business drastically, as the Kirkwood Drug Company moved in and would only offer a game of billiards and tobacco products instead of alcohol. The tavern and billiards industry was hurting badly between 1935 and 1957, leading to more fights, some fatal, inside and outside of the historic brick building.

In 1978, the Kirkwood Bar on the main level and Hinkles Lunch Restaurant upstairs had no choice but to close their doors when business declined drastically. The next year, the McConnaughy family saw potential in the building and purchased it, restored it and opened it back up in 1982. Today, the Irish Lion is a beloved tradition for family gatherings, holiday events and for those who, like the author of this book, want to experience their first alcoholic beverage on their twenty-first birthday. With so much history under one roof, it's not surprising that the famous restaurant and pub has a rich history of staff experiencing happenings they can't explain and didn't want to discuss until now.

The Irish Lion's web page says, "At closing, bartenders are asked to leave a shot of whiskey at the end of the bar to appease the departed," and briefly notes that there are many ghost stories. However, it also warns readers that these experiences may be the byproduct of one too many drinks. For Johnna Stepler, no drinks have been involved during any of the times she's experienced a handful of anomalies that she still wishes she had answers for. Johnna, who cleans the building in the early hours, around 5:00 a.m., is still confused when recounting the unexplained phenomena she saw.

Before any guests or staff members arrived one day, Johnna was working in the upstairs Celtic Room. While it's one thing to hear something or see something move out of the corner of one's eye, she "watched a wooden chair scoot across the wooden floor, about a foot in length, right in front of me." The moving chair was audible, since the move made the uncomfortable

Left: The upstairs area of the Irish Lion. The narrow, carpeted area on the far left is where the hotel hallways once stretched. On the ceiling, wood paneling shows where the hallway wall once stood, with the rooms to the right. *Author's collection, October 2020.*

Opposite: The downstairs area of the Irish Lion Pub. *Courtesy of the Irish Lion, 2021.*

sound of wood rubbing against wood. "I've also seen a chair turn in front of me about 30 degrees," she explained. Aside from seeing chairs move in the upstairs dining area, she has also seen a man or woman standing upstairs when no one else was in the restaurant. Johnna saw a dark figure standing right in front of her, but it wasn't a two-dimensional shadow. The figure was dark and three-dimensional, and there was no doubt that the person she was seeing was a real human being.

However, when Johnna flipped the light switch to on, the figure was nowhere to be seen. Shaken with terror, she ran away, bolted outside the building and immediately called her boyfriend to explain what had happened. On a separate occasion, Johnna and a coworker were in the downstairs bar area, chatting. During their talk, the two workers heard an ear-shattering crash directly above them. "Someone said the sound could've come from outside the building," Johnna recalls, "but we were

both saying, 'No. The sound definitely came from upstairs.' There was no doubt about that." The two girls ran up the stairs to see the origin of the loud crash. But as earsplitting as the sound was, the two employees found nothing knocked over or broken. There were no messes or items out of place anywhere upstairs.

THE WICKS COMPANY BUILDING AND THE HAUNTED ELEVATOR

116 West Sixth Street
Bloomington, Indiana

Directly across from the courthouse on Sixth Street, between North College Avenue and North Walnut Street, sits a towering building that is home to offices and small businesses. The impressive limestone building was constructed in 1915 in a Chicago Commercial style, making it the only one of its kind on the downtown square. The front façade of the three-story building is dominated by floor-to-ceiling windows, separated with a large panel of limestone above the first floor, which is engraved with the words, "The Wicks Company."

Although it's much smaller than the typical Chicago Commercial–style building, it reflects the basic architecture principles. The structure has a simple, rectangular shape and an entrance with a panel of leaded glass, which spans the length of the entire building. The corners of the building are made of wide piers of limestone, the ground floor consists of large display windows, and the second and third floors have narrower limestone piers, which divide the building into eight bays, with windows occupying the spaces in between. At the bottom of each window, there's a balcony or balustrade made of ornamental ironwork. The sides of the building are made of brick, the backside consists of standard windows on every floor and the exterior is painted brick. Overall, the structure is sound and in great condition.

Since it was erected in the early 1900s, the outside of the building hasn't received any major renovations, other than a minor one in 1995 to the first floor. In 2014, the upper two floors were renovated again to offer office spaces and areas for retail businesses. The limestone that was used for the Wicks Company Building, like all the others in the city of Bloomington, came directly from one of the local quarries. In fact, the original owner of the building was a Civil War veteran, Colonel W.W. Wicks, who became involved in limestone quarrying and later became interested in merchandise retailing.

Unfortunately, his first company building, one of the first department stores in Bloomington, was destroyed in a fire, and the Wicks family had to build the one that currently stands today. Their business remained opened until 1976 and is now the location for many office suites and local shops. The building itself is listed in the National Register of Historic Places, and it's part of the Courthouse Square Historic District. The large display window on the right side of the ground floor shows a nail salon, while the left display window allows people to view the inside of the Royal Hair Salon.

It's said that a hotel once operated in the Wicks Company Building, and the elevator was used to take guests between floors. The elevator was operated by an elevator hop, a person who was paid to push the buttons and stop the elevator at the exact time it reached the floor's landing. As soon as the elevator reached the floor, the button had to be pushed at the appropriate time, otherwise, the elevator would land too far above or below the floor, forcing the passengers to step up or step down from the elevator.

Madison, a hair stylist working at the Royal Hair Salon on the left side of the building, recalls creepy unexplained occurrences with the elevator. One night, Madison and a coworker stayed later than usual to do a color treatment on Madison's hair. While the other employees normally left around 8:00 p.m. every day, this hair appointment ran from 6:00 to 9:00 p.m., since color treatments typically take longer to perform than a haircut and styling. It was just the two girls in this part of the building. While Madison was seated in her coworker's station, they heard a strange, unfamiliar sound. The two stylists turned around to see the elevator directly behind them open its doors with no one inside. The doors stayed open briefly and then closed.

Just as the two ladies conversed about how strange it was and began to suspect an electrical issue, the elevator opened again to show, again, an empty compartment. "OK…" Madison and her friend noted, "That's probably just a coincidence." However, they were still unsure. Madison recalls discussing the situation with her other coworkers after that night, and one response she received was, "Well…we all kind of think it's haunted." Her coworker went on to explain that all of the stylists at Royal Hair Salon have had this same thing happen at some point, and although this sometimes happens during the day, it appears that the elevator operates on its own more frequently at night.

Another current employee of the salon has not only experienced the random opening and closing of the elevator, but they have also heard and even seen apparitions in the building. One of the figures she has seen is a bellhop, donned in his uniform, standing inside the elevator. She and other stylists have claimed to hear their name called when no one else was around. Usually, when the person turns around, there is no one in sight, and the person chalks the cause up to being tired. However, for one employee, they turned around after hearing their name and came face to face with a man who was clearly not a member of the living.

After seeing the man's apparition multiple times, Madison and her fellow stylist looked into the building's history. At the end of their research, the two firmly believed that the man the stylist had been seeing was the building's original owner, W.W. Wicks. Madison once thought she heard someone calling her name when she was alone; however, she saw no other person and believed she may have just been hearing things incorrectly. "Maybe someone is trying to grab our attention," says Madison, though she's not 100 percent certain. "It's bizarre, and it's definitely an interesting thing."

Possibly more unsettling than bizarre is one event that took place at night in the back room, where employees wash dishes, eat lunch and do laundry. Connected to the back room is a little hallway that leads into another back room, where many mannequins and mannequin heads are kept to allow stylists to practice their hair and makeup skills. One night, after closing, Madison was in the back room, waiting on her coworker to finish running the numbers at the front of the building so he could give her a ride after work. While she waited there, facing the hallway and the mannequin room, one of the mannequins in the dark room leaned forward on its own and fell to the ground. It was at that moment that she saw something move out of the corner of her eye. The light was off in the other room, and at the moment the mannequin landed on the floor, the lights flickered on and off. When the light flickered back off, Madison looked over at the light switch and saw that the switch was off, meaning there was no reason the light should have flicked on in the first place. It was at that point that Madison thought to herself, "OK…that's kind of freaky. I'm going to go," and went up to the front to look for her coworker.

"I thought that was weird," Madison later reminisced during an interview. When she was asked how she felt about the situation that occurred that night, she explained that she's not afraid of mannequins, since she practices on them 24/7, "but it tilted over and then fell on the ground. I looked over to see the light was off and just thought, 'Nope, nope, nope,' and left."

520 North Walnut Street and the Ghost Children

520 North Walnut Street
Bloomington, IN 47404

As a child, I spent a great deal of my time around downtown Bloomington. One of my parents worked on the square, I took music lessons, and my family and I would often have to pass through the downtown square to get somewhere. Like many parents, telling a story once was never enough for mine. Perhaps they forget that they've told their kids a story before, but it seemed like every time we drove up Walnut Street, I would receive the same, "See that house? It's haunted." While every time afterward, I responded with, "Yes, I know," the first time I heard the spooky tales of the old Walnut Street house, I remember looking up at my parents in eagerness, a twinkle in my bright little eyes, to hear more. That's when I learned of the two spirits of young children who are trapped inside. "Someone we know saw or heard them." Noises at night, a mysterious tunnel underneath the house and two little ghost children take center stage in this nineteenth-century home.

Walking north up Walnut Street, past all the little stone shops and the courthouse on the left, you'll arrive at a limestone home on your right at 520 North Walnut Street. Indiana is known as the Limestone State for its many limestone quarries. It is especially true for Bloomington, with its long history with the limestone industry, which the movie *Breaking Away* noted, as the Little 500 team from Bloomington was known as the "Cutters." Therefore, it's no surprise that this building, constructed in 1897 by Phillip K. Buskirk, is made with an all-limestone exterior. There are three floors, two of which are adorned by decorative limestone columns framing the entrance to the entrance on the first floor and four simple columns on the second floor.

It's evident that, even in this period, the owner of the house spared no expense, since there is also a thick, white trim with green ribbon-like design bordering the roof just under the first and second floors on the front and sides of the exterior. Facing the front of the home, there's an impressively large tree in the front and clean-cut hedges wrapping around the outline of the mansion.

Aside from the beautiful exterior, with the slate shingles and leaded glass, Phillip Buskirk added even more flair to the interior by adding somber oak woodwork to the railings and ornate structure of the rooms. On the first floor is a dining area, kitchen and a foyer. At the time the twelve-thousand-square-foot mansion was built, it was known as the most beautiful home in Bloomington. Unfortunately, the man was only able to enjoy his home for ten years before he died suddenly at the age of forty-four while eating at the dining table on August 22, 1907.

Like sundry old buildings around the city, the mansion fell into the hands of many families, businesses, a sorority and a fraternity. After Phillip's wife and son were no longer living in the home in 1910, the house was passed on to the Phi Beta Pi sorority. In 1925, it then became the

The 520 North Walnut Street mansion is no longer a private residence; however, it's still the place two ghost children call home. *Courtesy of Lauren Clark, 2021.*

home of the town's postmaster and president of Graham Motor Sales, William Graham. Between 1929 and 1945, the house became the home to yet another family—the Showers, who owned the large Showers Brothers Furniture business, which employed somewhere around 1,500 people. By the 1950s, the location became Phi Kappa Tau fraternity's house; then it was subdivided into office suites in 1965; and in the early 1970s, it was a restaurant named Whimples of Walnut Street. Throughout the decades, nothing suspenseful or out of the ordinary was recorded in the home. However, in the 1970s, when the home became the location of an Italian restaurant called Porticos, that all changed.

When the owners, Steve and Anita Lewallen, first purchased the building and started their Italian restaurant business, they had a sound-activated security system installed at every exit. The husband and wife eventually learned just how reliable their security system was, as they received a phone call at 3:00 a.m. from the alarm company regarding a sound within the restaurant that triggered the alarm, causing the authorities to arrive to investigate.

Although the police searched the entire home, top to bottom, there was no one in the building and no evidence of a break in, since all exits and windows were still closed and locked up. Even more confusing, the sounds that set off the alarm sounded like a ball being bounced around on the floor and the walls, accompanied by children saying, "Mommy, Daddy, come play with us." The police made sure to check each room and area of the old house where children could be hiding. None were found.

Guests dining at Porticos Restaurant were given the option to dine in either the dining room, probably the foyer on the first floor or upstairs, where Phillip and his wife's master bedroom once was. The story I remember hearing as a child—and that many in the community know—is that of two little children often spotted inside the restaurant. As my parents put it, a woman dining in the downstairs section left the table to use the public restrooms up the stairs on the second floor and then came right back to the table. On her return, she was either asked why she came back so quickly or went to confront one of the servers or owners.

"There are some children sitting on the steps with their arms locked, and they won't let me pass by," the lady said. Apparently, the children looked like real, living kids, since she was reported to not have acted alarmed in any way. When the servers and owners of the restaurant rushed to the stairs to find the kids, they couldn't find them. They searched the rest of the mansion again, and of course, the young kids weren't discovered anywhere.

In either an entirely different story or simply another version of the same story, a lady who had been dining at the restaurant went upstairs to the bathroom, but instead of running into two pesky youngsters waiting on the stairs, she was able to make her way all the way to the bathroom. Nevertheless, while she was inside the ladies' restroom, she could clearly hear kids laughing and playing in the next room. The woman exited the bathroom and went to the next room to see the kids, but once she entered, the noises stopped abruptly, and she found only an empty, lonely room. Reportedly, the woman was scared and started to second-guess what she had heard. Making her way back down the stairs to the rest of the dining area, she casually asked one of the waitresses if the children upstairs belonged to her or the owners. The server, understandably confused, advised the patron that the owners and staff didn't have any kids at the restaurant. "That's funny, because I heard children laughing upstairs," the woman replied. After hearing this, the waitress explained to the lady that she was not alone, laughing that the house was supposedly haunted, as numerous patrons had heard and sometimes seen these kids. The waitress, nevertheless, checked the rooms, which were inevitably empty.

It wasn't just the people eating there who reportedly heard and saw the apparitions. Staff members who have been interviewed for several newspapers over the decades have also claimed to have experienced similar phenomena with the ghost children. On one occasion, an employee was upstairs on the second floor, near the attic door, which had been closed at the time. While she stood there, she heard the distinct sound of a ball bouncing on the stairs on the other side of the attic door.

Too afraid to open the door and see what she might find, the employee left the area quickly. Another employee, a waitress, flew down the front stairway and into the foyer, panic-stricken, her face as white as a ghost, and crying. In a circumstance that sounds quite familiar to Stephen King's *The Shining*, the waitress had apparently been upstairs when she saw the two phantom ghost children standing in the hallway. She refused to go upstairs ever again, and another server had to cover the rest of her shift. The frightened employee never again went back upstairs during her employment at the restaurant.

Few know that, in the basement of the old mansion, there is a boarded-up wooden door that leads to an underground tunnel. This tunnel supposedly connects to the branching tunnel system under the city, which is probably connected to the tunnels that run throughout Indiana University's campus. Although we know for a fact that the tunnels are real, the reason they're there is still argued. One theory is that the tunnels were once used as part of the Underground Railroad.

It's been speculated that the sounds of the children are nothing more than what's being carried by the tunnels from a nearby place where children may be playing. However, there's no evidence that the tunnels go anywhere underneath a playground or schoolyard—now or when the restaurant was in business. Also, this theory is unlikely, since the door to the tunnel, which has remained closed and boarded up for decades, is in the basement, and people have clearly heard the kids upstairs, on the second and third floors.

If there are a couple of playful phantom children running around the stone manor, why have they been bound to this home for decades? It's thought that a farm stood where the building now stands, but the farm and the land surrounding it burned down long ago. Linda Degh, an IU folklore professor who wrote *Indiana Folklore: A Reader*, believes that, not two, but three young kids perished in the fire, which is why people have heard their screams on the second floor. In 1988, a local radio station host named Jerry Castor was inspired by Don Knott's movie *The Ghost of Mr. Chicken* to spend Halloween night by himself in the house. Jerry brought with him a tape recorder and slept in one of the rooms. He settled in for the night and didn't notice anything odd or out of place. There were no apparitions, no unexplained noises, no children.

During the night, while Jerry slept, his tape recorder remained running in order to capture any sounds. Although the radio host slept peacefully through the night, noises were picked up by the recorder. When the tape was replayed later, Jerry could be heard breathing heavily, and at one point, another sound could be heard faintly. Around 2:00 a.m., a child's voice was heard exclaiming what sounded like, "Go, Spot," "No, Spot," or something similar. Castor wasn't able to determine exactly what the voice was saying, and he claimed he didn't hear anything during the night. He did argue that it was unlikely there would be children awake and inside the house at 2:00 a.m.

It didn't take long for the community to spread the rumors of the two spirits that haunted Porticos, as there was an alarming number of people who had experienced run-ins with them. It's rumored that after a certain point, people were too afraid to eat at Porticos for fear of seeing the ghost children, supposedly causing the business to fail and leading to its permanent closure. The Porticos Italian restaurant has been closed for a long time and is now an attorney's office across from Dominos Pizza.

WYLIE HOUSE

307 East Second Street
Bloomington, IN 47401

The most recent phenomena at the Wylie House occurred in 2002, when two IU carpenter shop workers were rehanging some interior doors. Out of the corner of one his eyes, one worker spied a ghostly figure. Although he wasn't quick enough to see its facial characteristics, hair or age, he saw a woman standing near the parlor in a long yellow dress. The carpenter stopped his movements and said, "Who was that?" to his coworker. But when he turned to look, the woman was gone, and the room was empty. Although the carpenters were more curious than fearful, neither of them may have been aware of the house's long history with other nonthreatening haunts.

Built in 1835 and now an Indiana University–operated historical museum, depicting life in Bloomington around the 1840s, Wylie House was the home of IU's first president, Andrew Wylie, and his family. When the Hershey family moved into the house in 1913, the new owners discovered something strange. The house had yet to be finished, with some of the plastering remaining uncompleted. Confused as to why the Wylie family never finished plastering above the attic stairwell or near the attic door, the Hershey family investigated and discovered that the plasterer had stopped abruptly during

Wylie House. *Courtesy of* Travel with Sara, *April 30, 2018.*

his work when he received word that his wife had suddenly died. Distraught, the worker left immediately for home and committed suicide, either by hanging himself or jumping down a well.

The Hershey family completed the plastering in their new home; however, the lady of the house, Lillian Hershey, left the space above the attic stairwell unfinished out of respect for the plasterer. Although neighbors claimed that Mrs. Hershey wasn't fearful of ghosts or was said to believe in them, she chose not to sleep in the upstairs bedroom, just in case it was haunted. In 1986, when Mrs. Hershey's granddaughter Beth spent time in the Wylie House, she heard footsteps from the upstairs hallway—always around midnight.

Finally, Beth decided to sleep upstairs in the bedroom, probably in the hopes of investigating the sounds or that they may dissipate entirely with her sleeping up there. Yet, right on cue, like *The Ghost of Mr. Chicken*, a clock chimed, and Beth heard the footsteps descend the third floor, move down the hall and go down the main stairs. She believed the footsteps belonged to the spirit of the plasterer, who was walking the halls.

Footsteps in the upstairs hallway, along with other peculiar happenings, continued to be heard into the 1960s, when the house was undergoing major renovations. The IU campus police would receive calls of the lights being turned on when no one was in the house, and no sign of trespassing was found. On one occasion, one of the officers who was checking up on the house claimed to have been locked in the room on the second floor and heard footsteps running up to the third floor, toward the attic. Although the restoration supervisor, John Dixon, didn't believe in the ghost stories and feared nothing, his workers refused to work alone in a room.

Mr. Dixon changed his mind regarding the Wylie House when he heard a loud crashing from the kitchen. He hurried to the kitchen to find the empty room freezing cold with a turned over wheelbarrow and mortar dust clouding the air. Sometime later, a single brick was mortared into one of the interior walls of the home. This brick, found by Dixon and several other workers, had been cursed with a negative message regarding the Wylie family carved into it before being concealed within the wall.

Dixon, who was familiar with historic structures, noted that the brick wasn't a trick or a fake; it had been carved and mortared at the time the home was built. We never learned what exactly was carved into the brick, as Dixon smashed it with a hammer and claimed the message was too crude and inappropriate to be recorded in IU's archives. To this day, no one knows what curse was etched into the brick or if smashing it allowed the sounds to cease and any spirits to finally be at rest.

3

CEMETERIES

STEPP CEMETERY AND THE WOMAN IN BLACK

Myths which are believed in tend to become true.
—George Orwell

Stepp Cemetery
Martinsville, IN 46151

The most infamous cemetery and most haunted location in Indiana is a desolate cemetery tucked away in the Morgan-Monroe State Forest. Stepp Cemetery is also arguably one of the most haunted locations in the United States and is probably one of the creepiest, due to vandalism, purported occult rituals and an alarming number of witnessed hauntings—and for the simple fact that this is such an old, secluded cemetery. Located off of Old State Road, Stepp lies at the end of a tiny dirt road that leads back into the forest, where two dozen or so old and disintegrating grave markers remain, dating as far back as the early 1700s. It's a lonely little cemetery that receives few visitors these days, aside from those who love a good ghost story.

This resting place hasn't been the most restful in the past, due to the frequent disturbances from teenagers, religious or spiritual cults and troublemakers. To many people, Stepp Cemetery is a mystery, as

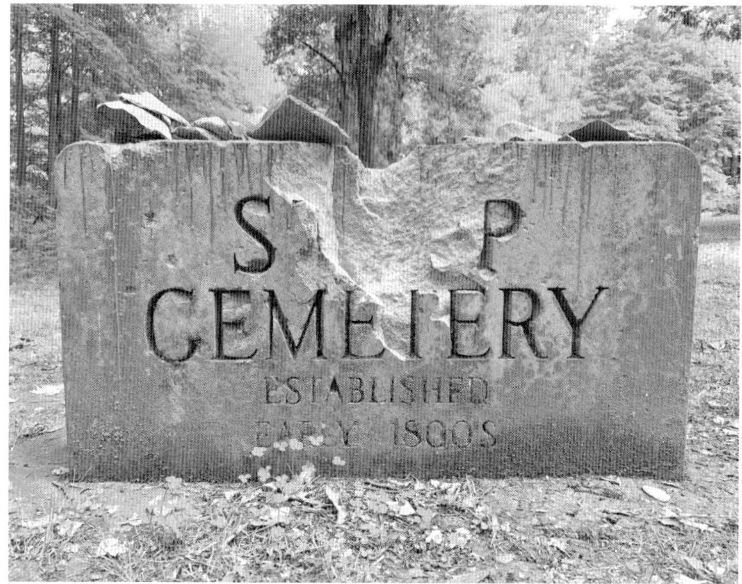

The Stepp Cemetery monumental sign, damaged by a gunshot and wax melted from magic rituals performed at the cemetery. *Courtesy of Paraholics, Indiana.*

many believe no one knows when or how the cemetery started. It's also been rumored that "Crabbites," a defunct religious cult that allegedly frequented the burial grounds in the past, created this cemetery. However, when one looks more into the history of this location, instead of believing the sensationalized legends, the rumor of the Crabbites establishing this cemetery turns out to be myth. Yet it's the countless legends and stories of strange and unusual occurrences with cults and ghosts that people know well.

Established in the early 1800s, Stepp Cemtery came from very humble beginnings, like nearly all of the historic locations in the state parks of Monroe County. The "Stepp" name comes from the old Stepp family. Reuben Stepp moved his family of nine from North Carolina to Monroe County and purchased the land in 1859. He built a corn and pig farm and a small cabin, which was used by the surrounding community as a church. Eventually, this wooden building began to rot and had to be torn down. At a certain point, as there were previously no cemeteries nearby, one had to be created for the Stepp family and the locals who resided nearby. The family eventually relocated to Texas, and over the next few decades, multiple families purchased and took over the land. In 1929, the

Morgan-Monroe State Forest was established to protect the forest from the increasing destruction happening across the area. Farmers were finding it increasingly hard to reap the rewards of their agricultural efforts, as there was a high amount of rock (most likely limestone) within the soil, creating a low-quality soil. This led the local farmers to tear down the woods in order to find soil of better quality.

While no one knows which religious groups or cults—besides the Crabbites—have visited the cemetery, the stories of cult-like happenings there are plentiful and span decades. Kristen from the *Journal of Folklore Research* at Indiana University admitted that she has visited multiple times during the daylight hours. This wasn't necessarily to avoid the ghosts—more so the people. Orgies, the destruction of tombstones and the angel statue, used candles from the previous night's rituals found on top of all the graves and the "Witch's Stump" and garbage thrown around the land have been reported over the years. Some of the ritualistic attempts have even been caught by other people and the authorities.

In tremendous disrespect to the memory of those who rest here, the headstones have been knocked over, moved from their burial plots and even removed completely from the cemetery, only to show up in parking lots and at a high school. While the tombstones are always moved back to their original plots, sometimes, the damage is irreversible, as the stones are a couple centuries old and have become broken or crumbled. All but one of the original grave markers have been defaced with spray paint, including the old statue of the angel that watches over the cemetery and the outside stone wall. One little gravestone that reads "BABY LESTER 1937" has had nearly all of its letters picked off. Visitors who come to pay their respects or to learn of the history of the area have even seen men urinating on the old tree stump that used to sit inside the cemetery walls.

Many paranormal research groups, such as Midwestern Researching, Indiana Ghost Trackers and Phantom Tribe, have visited Stepp over the years to try to witness the spirits that still lurk here. The most successful group was the Indiana Ghost Trackers from Indianapolis, who heard strange noises and footsteps inside the graveyard and captured photographs of a red glowing light source when flash wasn't used for the photograph. At one point, the group was standing in a circle when a couple of the members saw a white object inside their circle that then flitted outside of the circle and between the legs of one of the researchers.

What is the cause of all the paranormal research, destruction and increased interest in this humble, little cemetery for the last one hundred

The stump, or "Warlock's Chair," at Stepp Cemetery. *Courtesy of Paraholics, Indiana.*

years? The ghost stories are not only famous, but they stem from mystery and tragedy. There are many versions of a ghost story revolving around a ghostly lady who prowls this secluded part of these woods in the darkness, yet every version is similar in what the spirit does: mourn someone. She's called the Lady in Black, although she is different from the one who supposedly haunts downtown Bloomington. Some say this woman was murdered within the graveyard and is now confined to this part of the national forest for the rest of eternity. The ghostly woman, first witnessed in the 1950s, has been sighted by many who visit; they have seen her face appear in the windows of cars, possibly looking for her lost loved ones. Many have seen her sitting on a tree stump that resembles a seat, next to the tombstone belonging to a family member of hers with her face in her hands as if she's weeping.

This twisted tree stump has its own superstitious tales. "Warlock's Throne," "Warlock's Chair" and "Witch's Chair" are among a few of the names people have given this twisted stump over the years. Of course, this stump has since been removed, though many remember it well. Lightning supposedly struck this tree, creating the spooky stump. However, this is probably not how it was made, as one story involving the history of the farmland makes better sense. The Walls family who owned the land in the 1960s had to remove the tree due to it dying, yet they left the stump. Being the sawmill workers that the two brothers, William and Ralph, were, they formed it into the shape of a seat in case visitors wanted to use it to sit and relax while paying their respects.

It's also been said that they jokingly stated the seat could be used by the Lady in Black, since she often frequented the cemetery. The biggest superstition among teenagers and adults who have visited the cemetery claim that anyone who sits on the stump is cursed to die within the year. Some interpretations say that one needs to sit in the chair at midnight for the curse to take effect. Others have supposedly reported seeing a pair of gigantic black dog-like animals with glowing red eyes. The animals patrol the perimeter of the graveyard, sticking mostly to the wooded areas, but they enter the burial grounds to charge at those who intend to vandalize the cemetery.

Two brothers whose wealthy father had an estate either within or on the edge of the Morgan-Monroe State Forest were said to have quarreled with each other after their father's passing. In the heat of their disagreements, they held a duel within the forest, and after inflicting lethal blows to each other with their pistols, they both perished among the trees. People who

Baby Lester's grave is surrounded by toys, coins and other items. *Courtesy of Paraholics, Indiana.*

drive past both the Morgan-Monroe State Forest and the Hoosier National forest claim that their cars have suddenly died for no reason before starting back up after a few minutes. Because there's lacking evidence as to exactly which forest the wealthy family resided in, and due to the fact that both forests once had farmlands established near them, it's quite possible that the estate existed in either forest. Hikers who have visited these woods claim to have heard arguing, stumbled on the two brothers in the midst of their duel and seen the two men disappear once approached.

The little gravestone that gets the most attention in the cemetery has the words "BABY LESTER 1937" on it, and many think Baby Lester may be the son that the Lady in Black mourns. This is false, as Kristen from the *Journal of Folklore Research* at Indiana University states that the grave the ghostly lady keeps watch over belongs to her daughter. This variation in the story seems to be more accurate, as Baby Lester's mother, Olethia Walls, was discovered to be alive until she passed away in the early 2000s. Some people have claimed that they've witnessed the woman sitting down, cradling something in her arms or singing. This created the story of Baby Lester being the son of the female apparition, taken much too young. Baby Lester's grave sits in the corner, toward the back side of the graveyard, and has often been decorated with coins, combs, toys and other random items.

Stepp's Lady in Black is also thought to be a mother who died in a car accident with her young son. Yet another alteration of the story claims the woman's husband and young son were both killed in a car accident. The son and father perished and the mother survived, losing a hand in the process. The story gets a little more stretched, since it's said her hand was replaced with a silver hook, which she threatens visitors with if they dare to approach or disturb her son's grave. It's also promised that if someone places a penny on top of Baby Lester's grave, the invisible hand of his mother will knock the penny onto the ground right before their eyes. What we know to be true about little Lester is that he was sadly stillborn to Harley Lester and Olethia Walls in 1937, and when his mother was asked about the superstitions and myths surrounding her long-lost son before her passing at the age of eighty-five in 2007, she joked about having white hair but said she almost never wore black.

By far the most detailed legend surrounding the life of the phantom woman who now haunts the cemetery involves a woman, her husband and their daughter. Supposedly, the three moved to the area from the east, and the woman's husband had a job in one of the many quarries Bloomington is famous for. Sadly, the husband was killed during a dynamite explosion and buried in Stepp Cemetery. Stricken with grief, the woman put all her focus on her only child. As the daughter grew up, she remained very close to her mother. Unfortunately, the mother's grief returned when her daughter died in a car crash on a rainy night on her way back with her date from the spring dance at her school. It was a rainy night, like many spring nights, and the boy was rushing to return the girl home before her curfew. It's said that when the couple crashed, the girl's body was launched through the windshield, decapitating her. The daughter, like her father, was given a final resting place at Stepp Cemetery, and the mother vowed to wear only black from then on, thus giving her the name Lady in Black, as she is always witnessed in the cemetery donning a long black gown, with only her face and hands showing.

The devastated, lonely mother made nightly visits to the graveyard to sit near the graves of her departed family, where others would see her as they passed on the nearby road. After a while, it's said that people stopped visiting the little grave site, since the woman would be sitting there much of the time, including in the middle of the night. Locals referred to the poor lady as crazy, since anytime someone approached her, she would rise from the stump and flee into the forest, where she would hide until they left. According to legend, she was admitted to an asylum, possibly in Indianapolis, where the only one existed in the state at the time. Inevitably, the woman passed away and joined her family in the cemetery. But her spirit has remained restless. The stories that were to come from visiting the area and experiencing an encounter with the ghost woman are spooky to downright scary.

It's said her spirit is most active at night or during a full moon. According to Troy Taylor's *Beyond the Grave: The History of America's Most Haunted Graveyards*, people have left this graveyard "shaken" after seeing her in her black gown and long silver hair rise up from the tree stump and turn in their direction. Most likely since the 1950s, when most of the ghost stories started, many teenagers and probably college students would drive out to the state forest and park near Stepp Cemetery for some alone time. Some of these people have reported seeing the Lady in Black's face appear in the windows of their vehicles or knocking and scratching at the car doors, while other times, she's holding the bloody detached head of her beloved daughter.

It's possible the abundant stories are all from a few pranks that happened over the decades by several who have admitted to scaring people who went to the cemetery late at night. The local newspaper, the *Herald Times*, printed a story on August 30, 1966, about a couple of teenage boys who had hung a dog from a tree in the cemetery to scare others. They made the claim that they had found the already deceased dog before hanging it from a rope; however, they were still interrogated by authorities. It's not known what happened after their questioning, though it's most likely that nothing came of the situation.

The Lady in Black herself may actually be a man who lived in the 1960s by the name of John Findley. He also admitted to having spooked teenagers and adults alike with his friend Abram. In the summer of 1966, they created a trip wire system in which a bush would shake when the wire was tripped. The friends would then howl loudly. The two men even went as far as dressing a dummy in a black dress, hooking it to a pulley system and setting it inside the cemetery under a tree while they hid, waiting for a car full of teenagers. When everyone had exited their car, John and Abram would use the pulley system to make the dummy move toward the group. The two pranksters stated that the teens then jumped back into the car and sped off but not before one of the teens threw a soda bottle at the dummy. The Walls family, when they owned the land, admitted to hiding in the bushes to scare visitors in the dark.

Unfortunately, the Walls family regretted their actions, since these jokes only brought more trespassers and vandals to the area. So, while this little graveyard seems spooky, desolate and haunted by spirits, the stories are most likely the result of decades of pranks made by living, breathing people. If historians, teenagers and enthusiasts of spooky stories wish to pay Stepp Cemetery a visit, this can be done without defacing property and, instead, showing the deceased and the land the respect they both deserve.

Rose Hill Cemetery

1100 West Fourth Street
Bloomington, IN 47404

At South Elm Street and West Fourth Street, the Rose Hill Cemetery memorializes some of the most well-known Hoosiers. Right across the street are the best donuts you'll ever find at the historic Cresent Donut Shop and, legendary among Hoosiers, Hinkle's Hamburgers. Ghosts or no ghosts, the Rose Hill Cemetery is worth visiting. Hoagy Carmichael, a famous songwriter and singer who is still well known for composing "Heart

The gateway to Rose Hill Cemetery. *Courtesy of Matthew D. Jackson of Paraholics, Indiana.*

and Soul" and "Stardust," was buried here in 1981. Today, visitors continue to leave pennies in the grooves at the top of his tombstone. Famous jazz performers Daniel Kirkwood, for whom Kirkwood Avenue was named, and Elisha Ballantine of Ballantine Hall both have headstones here. Soldiers from the Revolutionary Wary, Civil War, Vietnam War and World War II are laid to rest here, as well as many prominent professors and figures from Indiana University, including the first president of IU, Andrew Wylie. Rose Hill is also the final resting place of twelve Bloomington mayors.

While it may be true that people today wouldn't choose a cemetery to spend a sunny afternoon in, graveyards were once the ideal place to take a peaceful walk and relax on a beautiful day because of their sprawling grounds, meandering pathways and flowers. Cemeteries are often lovely, wide-open spaces, as they were once originally parks, and they are still a great place to learn the history of a town. Centuries ago, it was completely normal to see people out with friends and neighbors in public graveyards, enjoying each other's company and fair weather.

The cemetery, which is one of the oldest in the city of Bloomington, has expanded greatly, since it was the first to be established around 1818. Before it was a cemetery, the land was considered out in the country; however, the city and the university were growing rapidly at the time, and a larger cemetery was needed. The southeast corner of the twenty-eight-acre graveyard, today, is the oldest part, with the earliest burial record dating back to October 6, 1897. Any other information regarding those buried here has to be collected from the headstones, newspaper articles and obituaries.

When Rose Hill was first created, it was only known as "Graveyard" and the letters "G" and "Y" were carved into the large oak tree that once stood at the entrance to let people know its location. Over time, the townspeople referred to the place as the "City Cemetery," and a stone entrance was added. Sometime between 1907 and 1927, the stone entrance was replaced by a concrete one with an iron gate. In 1892, a women's civil committee known as the Ladies' Cemetery Association took over the management of the graveyard and made improvements that we still enjoy to this day. The association planted an abundance of roses and renamed the cemetery "Rose Hill Cemetery" to give it a more appealing name. Benches, sidewalks and a crushed stone driveway were added. To make the grounds look even more appealing, they added a circular bed of pine trees and flowers around a stone fountain in 1893 in the center of the graveyard, which they called "Evergreen Arbor."

The Ladies' Cemetery Association did more than just update the overall appearance and give the location a more likable name. They also took the responsibility of marking and recording grave plots. The county also granted the association permission to hire a sexton, build a home on the grounds for him and have a salary of no more than $250 per year, which the city assisted in paying. Today, the large cemetery behind the stone wall is still serene and holds headstones made from the local limestone and red granite, as well as the first mausoleum in Southern Indiana, which was built in 1917. Some of the tombstones are shaped like tree trunks and are called "treestones." These became very popular in the Victorian era and come in a variety of styles—elaborate, simple, tall, short and with details and engraved epitaphs.

According to articles and interviews, it seems that the most paranormal hotspot of Rose Hill Cemetery is the Evergreen Arbor at the center of the graveyard. Those who are visiting loved ones have been said to experience a feeling of being watched or distinct cold spots. It seems the most common

Rose Hill Cemetery. *Courtesy of Matthew D. Jackson of Paraholics, April 2021.*

type of report is of shadow people darting between the trees or walking along the graves. These shadow people, which seem to be spotted around dusk, are said to be wearing Victorian garb and vanish into thin air when people notice them. Disembodied voices are heard calling to the living or whispering into their ears. While it seems like a cliché to see shadow figures or hear broken voices in a graveyard as night approaches, there are numerous reports of these events. An employee of Rose Hill Cemetery, however, said that the graveyard is pretty peaceful, and no one has been harmed by any ghosts here. The dead seem to be at rest.

Epilogue

Bloomington High School South (BHSS)

Bloomington High School South
1965 South Walnut Street
Bloomington, IN 47401

Experiencing a situation that feels perturbing or worrisome on your own isn't quite the same as experiencing that event with others. It's easy to write off an odd situation as nothing more than one's mind or eyes playing tricks. However, when something unusual and unexplained happens in the presence of another person, it's hard to argue the phenomena didn't happen.

I attended BHSS with an impressive glass atrium at the front of the building—the location of the school's annual prom. The atrium features steps that allow access to the second and third floors, with the stairs sweeping gracefully down to the first floor at the entrance of the glass windows and doors that make up the atrium. The second floor gives access to the Carmichael Auditorium to the right and the library and classes up the steps to the left. The third floor leads to more classes and the school's bookstore under the last and highest set of stairs, which leads to more classes. Aside from the atrium area and a separate B wing, the main building of the school sits in an almost-square shape in all three floors.

I always acted in theater in high school, while my best friend would opt to be a backstage grip. After rehearsal, my parents would pick us up. When rehearsals ran late one night, the sky was dark outside, and the school was devoid of students and faculty. Walking out of the auditorium and into the theater's lobby to leave, my friend froze in her tracks, stating she forgot her belongings backstage. I needed my backpack from my locker, so we agreed to reconvene somewhere in the middle after retrieving our things. She reentered the auditorium, and I made my way to the opposite end of the desolate school to my locker.

As I rummaged through my locker, I experienced a strong, uncomfortable feeling of being watched. I stopped and slowly turned to my right, toward the end of the hallway. At least a few feet off the tiled floor was a pitch-black formless mass hovering by the corner of the wall where the two hallways intersected. The border of the mass seemed to be flowing like a moving liquid or a mist. The outline of it was impossible to determine. It wasn't a solid line, but it had tendrils coming out of it in every direction, which were larger toward the middle of the creature and gradually became thinner toward the tips. As unsettling as this image sounds, these tentacle-like wisps were twirling and writhing around in every direction, with the focal point of the creature hovering absolutely stationary. The creature wasn't just black—it was completely void of any color. Scientists have created a substance that is blacker than anything we have been able to see, and this thing that was watching me was impossibly black. There were no facial characteristics or limbs.

The creature seemed to be watching me silently as I went through my locker, but when I turned, it flew away. Instead of vanishing, it swept through the air behind the corner of the intersecting hallways, its vapor-like tendrils flying behind it. It was almost as if it didn't want to be seen. I didn't stick around or follow it, since it gave me a negative vibe. I shut my locker and ran back to the auditorium—not once looking behind me.

I burst through the doors, into the theater lobby, and nearly ran headfirst into my friend, who was running fast toward the exit. I didn't plan on giving any explanations but was about to tell her that we had to leave fast. However, I wasn't given the chance, as she abruptly demanded, "We need to leave, NOW." I froze for a second with a puzzled face, so she began to quickly stumble over her words, moving her hands around in the air, attempting to desperately explain that she had seen something and didn't know what it was. Frantic, she began, "I saw something—"

"Was it black?" I interrupted. She froze again with a horror-stricken expression.

Motionless and gaping, she nodded slowly. "Yes…and it had these…*things* coming off of it—" moving her hands and fingers as if pulling apart taffy apart. "Yes," I agreed, "and it floated." We stood staring at each other and agreed to leave immediately. There was no agreement or pact between us; we simply never discussed that night again. This unsettling experience is one I've carried alone for decades, afraid of skepticism. The internet holds no explanation for what I saw that night, nor any information of others witnessing something similar. I've never found my answer, but I remember how I felt the moment I realized something was watching me. I've always wondered if I would see it again one day. I have yet to. The odd belief I can't seem to shake is that I will, eventually, have to see it again.

Bibliography

Alpha Phi. "About Us." www.betatau.alphaphi.org.

Anders, Caroline. "Secrets of the Herman B Wells Statue." *Indiana Daily Student*, March 1, 2018.

Baker, Tom. "My Bloody Boneyards." 2018. Horror. www.vocal.media.com.

Briscoe, Bailey. "Beck Chapel: Steeped in More Than 60 Years of History." *Campus Life*, August 7, 2017.

Brodsy, Alyson, and Alexis Silas. "Spirits Abound on Campus." *Indiana Daily Student*, October 31, 2000.

Callanan, Liam. "*The Cloud Atlas* Quotes." October 26, 2004. www.goodreads.com.

Coley, Craig. "Rose Hill Cemetery Bicentennial; A Brief History and Curious Facts." February 5, 2019. www.magbloom.com.

Dickinson, Emily. *The Complete Poems of Emily Dickinson*. Boston: Little, Brown, 1924.

Fernando, Christine. "Haunts." *812*, n.d. www.812magazine.com.

———. "The Woman in Black and Other Ghosts Haunt IU's Campus." *Indiana Daily Student*, April 19, 2018. www.idsnews.com.

Find a Grave. "Rose Hill Cemetery" www.findagrave.com.

Freiberg, Chris, and Sills C. Warner. "School Spirit…Haunted Since 1820." *Indiana Daily Student*, October 29, 2003.

Haack, Allison. "Ghost Stories from Wylie House." October 25, 2013. www.wyliehouse.wordpress.com.

Haas, Katelyn. "Dunn Cemetery Sits on IU's Campus Quietly but Speaks of History." *Indiana Daily Student*, October 30, 2017.

Hinton, Rick. "Urban Legends: The Vanishing Hitchhiker, Graveyard Watcher and Ladies in Black or White." *Southside Times*, March 12, 2020.

Horn, Dave. "Bloomington's Premier Haunted House." August 18, 2018. www.hoosiertimes.com.

Huffine, Natalie. "I Went on the Bloomington Ghost Walk and Now I'm Too Scared to Go to the IMU." *Tab*, 2017.

Indiana Memorial Union Facebook page. October 9, 2019. www.facebook.com.

———. October 31, 2019. www.facebook.com.

Indiana Memorial Union website. "A History 100+ Years in the Making." www.imu.indiana.edu.

Irish Lion. "History of Bloomington and Monroe County." www.irishlion.com.

———. "History of the Irish Lion." www.irishlion.com.

Johnston, Courtney. "The Sinister Story Behind This Popular Indiana University Will Give You Chills." August 18, 2017. www.onlyinyourstate.com.

———. "These 8 Haunted Cemeteries in Indiana Are Not For the Faint of Heart." July 20, 2016. www.onlyinyourstate.com.

Keck, Mary. "IU Bloomington Considered One of the Most Beautiful College Campuses in U.S." March 29, 2017. www.news.iu.edu.

Kenney, Marky. "Stepp Cemetery Haunted By 'the Woman in Black.'" *Indiana Daily Student*, October 29, 2010.

Klockow, Kat. *Haunted Hoosier Halls: Indiana University*. Atglen, PA: Schiffer Publishing, August 10, 2010.

Krause, Carrol. "Bloomington's Old Presbyterian Farmhouses." *Herald-Times*, April 19, 2014. www.heraldtimesonline.com.

Ksander, Yaël. "Stepp Cemetery." October 22, 2007. www.indianapublicmedia.org.

Lake, Tyler. "Stepp: A Small Rural Cemetery That Looms Large in Hoosier Lore." October 26, 2018. www.indianapublicmedia.org.

Leeds, Griffin. "Ballantine Stairs Explained." *Tab*, 2015.

Ley, Jan. "Brave Sisters Helped Militia Men—Right Next Door: Daughters of the American Revolution." July 17, 2000. www.cwcfamily.org.

Mack, Robert. "Learn About Some of IU's Statues and Their History." March 1, 2018. www.idsnews.com.

Marimen, Mark. *Haunted Indiana*. Tales of the Supernatural Series 1. West Branch, MI: Thunder Bay Press, June 1, 1997.

Matson, Donals. "Rose Hill Cemetery." www.bloomington.in.gov.

McCarthy, Kayla. "True or False? Myths of IU, the Dunn Family." *Pride of IU*, January 20, 2018. www.pride.iu.edu.

Mercedes, Christina. "5 Famous IU Spots and the Origin of Their Names." October 27, 2016. www.weareiu.com.

News at IU. "A Sampling of Quotes from Past Inaugurations." April 9, 2004. www.newsinfo.iu.edu.

Orwell, George. "The English People" In *The Collected Essays, Journalism and Letters of George Orwell*, 144. Vol. 3. Edited by Sonia Orwell and Ian Angus, 1968.

Parfitt, Mark. "Did You See *Oprah*?" October 30, 1998. www.collegian.psy.edu.

Reitman, Ivan, dir. *Ghostbusters*. Film. Culver City, CA: Columbia Pictures, 1984.

Santagata, Cindy. *Indiana Daily Student*, November 1, 1989.

Sculptureworks. "Tuck Langland 'Herman B. Wells' Monument." www.sculptureworks.com.

Sidney and Lois Eskenazi Museum of Art. www.artmuseum.indiana.edu.

Sylvester Floyd, Katheryn, and Mary Quilter. "GHOSTS and GOBLINS; They May Not Get You but Watch Out." *Indiana Daily Student*, October 31, 1984.

Taylor, Troy. *Beyond the Grave: The History of America's Most Haunted Graveyards*. Alton, IL: Whitechapel Productions, January 1, 2001.

Tripadvisor. "Wylie House Museum." www.tripadvisor.com.

Wallace, Dylan. "IU's Paranormal Activity Occurs at Most Popular Campus Locations." October 24, 2018. www.idsnews.com.

Willis, James A. *Haunted Indiana: Ghosts and Strange Phenomena of the Hoosier State*. Haunted Series. Mechanicsburg, PA: Stackpole Books, February 16, 2012.

Interviews

Anderson, Madison. Personal Interview [phone conference] at the Royal Hair Salon. November 26, 2020.

Downs, Kristina, PhD. Personal interview [phone conference] at the *Journal of Folklore Research*. September 2020.

MacDonald, Megan. Personal Interview [phone conference] at the Monroe County Historical Center. November 2020.

Stepler, Johnna. Personal interview [phone conference] at the Irish Lion. September 2020.

About the Author

Rock and roll drummer, coffee addict and horror movie enthusiast, Klara Lee Sweet travels as frequently as possible with her husband throughout the United States and overseas. On each adventure, they enjoy ghost tours and collecting folklore stories. Books in Klara's personal collection include Stephen King's novels, 1980s rock and roll autobiographies, cozy mysteries and Haunted America Series books she's collected on her travels. *Haunted Bloomington, Indiana* is the first book Klara has written or published. A proud Hoosier, this was her way of helping local businesses—educating others of the hometown she loves dearly.